TOM THUMB

The Remarkable True Story of a Man in Miniature

GEORGE SULLIVAN

CLARION BOOKS
Houghton Mifflin Harcourt
Boston New York 2011

CLARION BOOKS

215 Park Avenue South, New York, New York 10003

For information about permission to reproduce selections from this book, write to
Permissions, Houghton Mifflin Harcourt Publishing Company,
215 Park Avenue South, New York, New York 10003.

Clarion Books is an imprint of
Houghton Mifflin Harcourt Publishing Company.

www.hmhbooks.com

The text was set in Abrams Venetian.
Book design by Christine Kettner

LIBRARY OF CONGRESS CATALOGING-IN-PUBLICATION DATA

Sullivan, George.
Tom Thumb : the remarkable true story of a man in miniature / by George Sullivan.
p. cm.
ISBN 978-0-547-18203-2
1. Thumb, Tom, 1838-1883. 2. Dwarfs—Biography. I. Title.
GN69.3.S85 2010
791.092—dc22
[B]
2009052910

Manufactured in Singapore
TWP 10 9 8 7 6 5 4 3 2 1
4500262743

CONTENTS

Introduction

IN 1863, AS THE CIVIL WAR was approaching its midpoint and the North still agonized over its disastrous defeat in Virginia at Fredericksburg, an unusual event crowded all news of the conflict off the front pages of many newspapers across the nation. It was a wedding that took place early in the afternoon of February 10, at Grace Episcopal Church in New York City.

The groom was twenty-five-year-old Charles S. Stratton, two feet, eleven inches in height and known professionally as Tom Thumb. His bride was Lavinia Warren, four years younger and an inch shorter than Charles. The *New York Times* called her the "Queen of Beauty."

On the day of the wedding, Grace Church was filled to overflowing, and an enormous crowd gathered in the streets outside. Police

A wedding in miniature. ✦ *Author's collection*

1

put up barricades and formed human chains in an effort to control the throng. New York's wealthiest and most notable families—the Vanderbilts, the Astors, and the Belmonts—were among those who attended.

After the ceremony, done "decently and in order," according to the *Times,* hundreds of people chased the wedding carriage to the Metropolitan Hotel, where the reception was to be held. There, standing atop a grand piano, Tom and Lavinia received more than two thousand guests.

At the time of the wedding, Tom Thumb was already a superstar, his name a household word in America and Europe. As a result of his personal appearances at Phineas T. Barnum's American Museum in New York and his European travels, Tom was beloved the world over and had amassed a good-size fortune. He owned a dazzling yacht, a stable of fine horses and carriages, and a magnificent home. He dressed in the finest clothes and enjoyed rich food and expensive cigars.

Tom Thumb, in fact, was the nation's first celebrity. There were famous people before him, of course—such as Benjamin Franklin, Aaron Burr, and Samuel F. B. Morse. But no actor or stage perform-

Very early in what would be a long relationship, Tom Thumb and P. T. Barnum became quite fond of each other, an attachment reflected in this chummy photograph.
✦ *Bridgeport Public Library Historical Collection*

er, no musician, athlete, or other professional had ever commanded the public attention the way Tom did. No one in the world was as widely known or as successful.

Tom Thumb's celebrity status was due in no small measure to Barnum. It was Barnum who taught Tom to be a performer—to sing, dance, mime, and impersonate famous people. It was through Tom's shows at Barnum's American Museum, the Disney World of its time, that Tom first came to the public's attention.

To publicize Tom and his stage appearances, Barnum provided a never-ending stream of handbills, posters, and newspaper articles about Tom and his activities. "Barnum was a genius in promotion," according to Kathy Maher, the executive director of the Barnum Museum in Bridgeport, Connecticut. "People ask me what he would be today. He would be Disney and Donald Trump combined."

Tom toured western Europe with Barnum several times and performed for the crowned heads of England, France, and Spain. Later, Tom and his wife and their theatrical company presented shows in Europe, Asia, and Australia, on a tour that lasted three years.

Of course, it wasn't only people with dwarfism whom Barnum and other showmen of the time put on public display. The very tall ("Giants"), the unusually skinny ("Human Skeletons"), the obese, those with uncommon skin disorders ("The Amazing Alligator Woman") or excessive body hair ("Jojo, the Dog-Faced Boy"), and people with extra limbs were also exhibited as human oddities.

Even today, people with dwarfism can find employment in freak shows at New York's Coney Island, as evidenced in this 2009 photograph. ✦ *George Sullivan*

During the nineteenth century people with such physical differences were commonly referred to as freaks of nature, or simply freaks. Freak shows were a regular feature at carnivals and circuses, and an accepted part of American life.

Changes in popular culture eventually led to the decline of freak shows as a form of entertainment. Today, freak shows, though they still exist, are rare. In several states they are outlawed. The general public has come to look upon dwarfs differently too. Television, films, and cyberspace have provided a more well rounded and respectful view of people of short stature. Organizations such as Little People of America have won greater dignity and more of an equal place in society for their members. Many more opportunities in the professional world are now available to LPs (little people) as a result.

But for Tom Thumb, there were very few choices. As a five-year-old, he was made into a show business performer by Barnum, and he remained in that role all his life.

CHAPTER ONE

A Man in Miniature

 LOVE TO WATCH children play," General Tom Thumb once remarked to his wife as he neared middle age. "I never had much childhood."

It's true. Tom's career in show business began abruptly, just before his fifth birthday, under P. T. Barnum's direction. From the beginning, Tom was taught to act like an adult because Barnum wanted to create the idea that he was more grown up than his looks indicated. Barnum felt this would add to his performer's appeal. Tom had to learn to speak like an adult, too, despite his high and squeaky voice.

At five, Tom was drinking wine with his meals. At seven, he smoked cigars. By nine, he chewed tobacco. He never had a day of school.

General Tom Thumb was the boy's stage name, given to him by Barnum. He

was born Charles Sherwood Stratton on January 4, 1838, in Bridgeport, a seaport town in Connecticut. His mother called him Charley. He weighed nine pounds, two ounces, which was large for a newborn. His sisters, Frances June, four years old when Charley was born, and Mary Elizabeth, two, had not weighed that much at birth.

With two girls already in the family, the Strattons were thrilled to have a

Charley was born and raised in this Bridgeport home, along with his older and average-size sisters, Mary Elizabeth and Frances Jane, nicknamed Libbie and Jennie.
✦ *Bridgeport Public Library Historical Collection*

boy. Mrs. Stratton showered him with thoughtful care. She was grateful to have a healthy baby.

At first, Charley grew normally. By the time he was six months old, he weighed fifteen pounds, two ounces. He was twenty-five inches long. But as time passed, lines of worry began to crease Mrs. Stratton's face. Charley seemed to stop growing. By his first birthday, he still weighed fifteen pounds, two ounces and was twenty-five inches long, exactly the same size he had been six months earlier.

Mrs. Stratton thought perhaps she wasn't giving Charley the right food or enough of it. But getting Charley to eat more didn't solve the problem. There was not the slightest change in his height or weight.

Nothing in the Stratton family history provided a clue to Charley's lack of growth. Mr. and Mrs. Stratton were of average height and weight, as were their parents, Charley's grandparents.

Once it was obvious that Charley had stopped growing, his parents took him to their family doctor. After he had examined the child, the doctor shook his head, perplexed. Charley was a healthy baby and seemed to be developing normally in all other ways.

He was also perfectly formed. His arms and legs were in proportion to the rest of his body.

Why was Charley so tiny? The doctor had no answer.

At the time, medical authorities had only a limited knowledge of the factors important to human growth. It would be another fifty years before they would begin to understand the role played by the pituitary gland, a pea-size endocrine gland that rests within a bonelike cavity at the base of the brain.

Healthy and bright-eyed Charley, with his father, Sherwood, a carpenter, and his mother, Cynthia, who worked at a Bridgeport inn. ✦ *Charles Schwartz Photography*

Sometimes called the body's "master gland," the pituitary governs the body's growth. In Charley's case, it is now thought that the pituitary gland failed to function properly, resulting in a deficiency of the growth hormone it normally produces.

Today, if a child fails to grow normally, the pituitary gland can sometimes be treated to trigger growth. Injections of HGH, human growth hormone, during the early years can increase a child's height. If it had been possible for Charley to have been treated with HGH, chances are he would have grown taller, perhaps even to average height. But in the 1830s, doctors could do nothing when confronted with a child who did not grow normally.

Charley's mother and father had their own explanation for their son's size. Mr. and Mrs. Stratton, like many people in Victorian times, believed in "maternal impression." According to this theory, if a pregnant woman is exposed to an event that causes her severe stress, the form of her child could be affected in some way.

The idea of maternal impression has a long history. In ancient Greece, for example, a pregnant woman would be made to stare at statues of strong and handsome figures. Doing so, it was believed, would cause her child to have these traits. A woman who happened to bear an unattractive child could be accused of neglecting her statue-staring duty.

❍ ❍ ❍ ABOUT DWARFISM ❍ ❍ ❍

Dwarfism is any condition of short stature that has resulted from a medical or genetic condition and is defined as an adult height of four feet, ten inches or less. The proper term for a person of short stature is "dwarf" or, preferably, "little person." The term "midget" is considered offensive.

There are more than two hundred types of dwarfism. The most frequent type is achondroplasia, a genetic condition that accounts for about 70 percent of cases of short stature and results in disproportionate dwarfism, in which the body size is average but arms and legs are truncated. Other forms of disproportionate dwarfism may result in a short trunk as well as shortened arms and legs.

Charley Stratton's short stature was the result of "proportionate dwarfism," in which all parts of the body are in the same proportion as those of an average-size person, just smaller. Proportionate dwarfism is most commonly caused by a deficiency in human growth hormone, a chemical produced by the pituitary gland. It is thought that this was the cause of Charley's small size, but of course it is impossible to say for sure, as the medical tools for diagnosis did not exist during his lifetime. It is quite possible that if Charley had lived in modern times and could be treated with hormone therapy, he would have grown to an average size.

More information on dwarfism is available from Little People of America (www.lpaonline.org), a support organization for people of short stature and their families.

❍ ❍ ❍ ❍ ❍

Not long before Charley was born, the Stratton family's black and tan puppy drowned in the river that flowed behind their house. Terribly grief-stricken at the loss, Mrs. Stratton wept hysterically. The Strattons believed this tragic event and Mrs. Stratton's reaction to it caused her baby to be "marked." The mark was Charley's tiny size.

When their doctor could offer no hope that Charley would ever reach anything near normal height, the Strattons were forced to admit that their son was a dwarf. The thought that Charley would be so physically different from other children filled them with dismay.

Mrs. Stratton, who blamed herself for Charley's condition, came to have a fierce love for her son. She felt a strong urge to protect him from the teasing of other children and the open-mouthed stares of adults.

When Mrs. Stratton and Charley walked down the streets of Bridgeport, people would point and gape. Sometimes they would even call out, "Hey, look at that midget!" or make other thoughtless remarks. To avoid such incidents, or anything that might her son feel uncomfortable, Mrs. Stratton sometimes carried Charley about in a market basket, covering him with a small blanket.

Charley's father, Sherwood Stratton, a carpenter, loved his son too, but he could not help feeling upset and embarrassed when townspeople gawked at Charley in shops or on local streets. His Stratton forebears had been robust and

strong-willed people. Many of the men had served in the military. Mr. Stratton sometimes felt that he and his wife were victims of some kind of cruel joke.

As for Charley himself, his short stature caused him none of the inner turmoil that his parents suffered. Of course, he realized he was different from other children. But he only felt smaller; he did not feel handicapped in any way.

Like any young child, Charley simply learned to cope with the fact that everything in the world was designed for people who were bigger and taller. He got accustomed to standing on a wooden box to reach the kitchen sink. When he couldn't get to an object on a high shelf, he'd climb onto a chair or ask for help. He learned to sit near the edge of chairs so his legs wouldn't stick out awkwardly.

Charley fascinated grownups. In any group of adults, he was the center of attention. Whereas this situation might have made some children uncomfortable, Charley seemed to revel in it.

He soon developed an impish, rough-and-tumble nature and capitalized on his size in order to cause mischief. He would disappear under furniture to torment his parents. Kitchen cabinets and the family soup tureen were among his favorite hiding places. Visitors to the Stratton home were startled when Charley suddenly streaked between their legs or plunked himself into their laps.

Sherwood Stratton loved his son dearly but became ill at ease when the child stopped growing. ✦ *Bridgeport Public Library Historical Collection*

Since Charley seemed so completely unbothered by his size—he even seemed to get a certain joy out of it—his parents' feelings began to change. Their discomfort and shame lessened. Little by little, they learned to accept the fact that their son was never going to be much bigger than any of the dolls their daughters played with.

His father put his carpentry skills to work to fit the house with furniture suited to Charley's size. Although Charley had never outgrown the cradle he had used as an infant, his father made him a bed of his own, one with a tiny headboard and mattress. His mother, using scraps of cloth, crafted sheets, blankets, and a bedspread.

Mr. Stratton also made Charley his own chest of drawers, which was about the size of a milk crate. The boy got his own wooden chair and table too.

Once his parents let go of their fears that Charley would be ridiculed, he soon became a well-known curiosity in Bridgeport. People in the small city relied primarily on fishing and farming for their income. Extra men were always needed to work the farms during the fall harvest, so neighbors assembled at one another's homes to help out. When the ripe crops had been gathered, the families would celebrate by dancing, footracing, and wrestling. Charley's parents often took him to such events. Filled with glee, he would run about under tables and chairs, pinching the legs of other children. He took a special pleasure in kissing little girls, although he sometimes had to stand on a stool to do so.

The Strattons were friendly with Henry Seltsem, Bridgeport's "Dutch baker," a man who guided his horse-drawn wagon from house to house through the streets, selling his breads and pastries to local housewives. One of Charley's great delights was to be invited to ride in the driver's seat next to Mr. Seltsem on his daily journey.

Bridgeport in 1837, the year before Charley's birth. ✦ *Bridgeport Public Library Historical Collection*

Bridgeport had recently become a stop on the Housatonic Railroad. Trains from the city now operated to and from Albany, New York, and the Berkshire Hills in Massachusetts, both to the north.

Most people, however, still used the stagecoach for overland travel. Stagecoach passengers often stayed and took their meals at the Sterling House, a hotel on Main Street in Bridgeport. Charley's mother often worked there, helping out with the cooking and cleaning.

Mrs. Stratton sometimes brought Charley with her when she went to work. He became a favorite of the Sterling House clerks, cooks, and waitresses. Because of all the attention he received, and his playful pranks, dinner was often late at the Sterling House when Charley visited.

Seated on a high stool, Charley sometimes dined with the hotel guests. They marveled at his big appetite.

One winter day at the Sterling House, Theodosia Fairchild, the wife of the hotel manager, rushed in to tell Mrs. Stratton what she felt was very exciting news.

"He's here!" she said. "He's here!"

"Who is?" asked Mrs. Stratton.

"P. T. Barnum," Mrs. Fairchild answered.

Everyone knew Phineas Taylor Barnum. He had recently purchased Scudder's American Museum on Broadway in New York City and renamed it after

himself. He was known to be seeking new acts for his enterprise. In time, Barnum would become the greatest showman of the nineteenth century. No one would do more to amuse and entertain people of the day.

Mrs. Fairchild explained that Mr. Barnum had been in Albany on business. When he set out to return to New York City by boat, he found that the Hudson River was frozen over. He then took the Housatonic Railroad to Bridgeport. Mrs. Fairchild went on to report that Mr. Barnum was staying at the Franklin House, another Bridgeport hotel, which was managed by Philo T. Barnum, his half brother. Charley's mother sometimes helped out with the cleaning at the Franklin House as well.

Mrs. Stratton knew why Theodosia Fairchild was so excited. She had often spoken to Mrs. Fairchild about Charley and the difficult life he would face as an adult. How would he cope with the jeering and taunting? How would he be able to support himself? And what about marriage? How would he ever find someone who would be interested in him romantically?

Barnum, according to Theodosia Fairchild, represented an opportunity for Charley, a chance to break free from the difficult life he faced. She urged Mrs. Stratton to put her son in Barnum's hands.

"No, I can't," said Mrs. Stratton.

Mrs. Stratton knew all about P. T. Barnum and the life he would offer her

son. Earlier in the year her mother had gone to New York and while there had paid a visit to Barnum's grand showplace, the American Museum. She returned to describe what she had seen.

There were all kinds of special shows and contests—flower shows, dog shows, and bird shows. There were baby shows, with cash prizes for the brightest, prettiest, and fattest infants.

Jugglers, ventriloquists, and magicians performed. One of the leading attractions was Robert Hales, who was seven and a half feet tall and weighed over 450 pounds. There was also a giantess, Eliza Simpson, who was almost as big. After Robert and Eliza fell in love, Barnum arranged for the pair to get married at the museum, an event he charged the public to attend.

Dwarfs were among Barnum's first successful human exhibits. When Mrs. Stratton's mother visited the museum, "Major" Stevens was the featured dwarf. The son of a cobbler, and one of the first American dwarfs ever exhibited, Stevens was now forty years old and thirty -seven inches tall, just over three feet.

Barnum realized people in the northeast United States were fascinated by Native Americans, so he hired a small band of Iowa Indians to perform tribal dances for his customers. They lived on the fifth floor of the museum, where

Opened on New Year's Day, 1842, Barnum's American Museum on Broadway in New York City became a hugely popular entertainment center, the Disney World of its day.
✦ *Barnum Museum*

they cooked their meals in the fireplace and slept on the floor.

The museum also offered Isaac Sprague, who, at forty-three pounds, was billed as "The Living Skeleton." R. O. Wickware, whose body was so thin that strong rays of light could be seen through it, was advertised as "The Living Phantom." S. K. Nellis, an armless performer, played the accordion with his toes.

After her mother recited all that she had seen, Mrs. Stratton made up her mind. She would never allow Charley to be exhibited among such people.

That didn't matter to Mrs. Fairchild. "I'm going straight over to Franklin House," she announced, "and tell Philo Barnum he must have his brother take a look at Charley."

Mrs. Stratton winced. "Oh, please don't!" she said.

"Yes, I must," Mrs. Fairchild said. With that, she snatched up her coat and hurried off to the Franklin House.

That evening at home, Mrs. Stratton recounted the day's events to her husband. When she told him that Mrs. Fairchild thought P. T. Barnum might want to show Charley at his museum in New York, Mrs. Stratton was surprised to see her husband's face brighten at the news. He seemed very pleased.

Her daughters too. They made no effort to hide their delight. From the time it was realized that he was a dwarf, Charley had made the two girls feel uncom-

fortable. They wondered how he was going to be treated once he started school. How would he fit in? Would he be an embarrassment to them? If he were to leave for New York, they could be relieved of that worry.

Later that evening, when Philo Barnum called upon the Strattons, he greeted Mrs. Stratton warmly. Taking off his coat, hat, and scarf, he glanced about the room and spotted Charley seated in the tiny chair his father had made for him. He had never seen Charley before. He walked over to the boy, then bent down and eyed him closely.

"Remarkable," Mr. Barnum said. "Taylor [Phineas Taylor—P. T.] won't believe this," he added. "You know, he wants to see your son."

"But, Mr. Barnum, you might as well know I'm not at all in favor of any of this," said Mrs. Stratton.

Philo Barnum tried to persuade her. He said, "Think what it will mean to your son." He explained that if his brother exhibited Charley at his museum, the boy—and his family—could become rich and famous.

Mrs. Stratton was unmoved. Charley, she said, "was not an object just for a museum."

Her husband felt differently. "What did you say about Charley's becoming rich and famous?" he asked.

Philo Barnum nodded. "And make you rich, too," he said.

Mr. Stratton turned to his wife. "At least let's go and talk to Mr. Barnum," he said.

So it was agreed. Mrs. Stratton wrapped Charley in warm blankets, and Mr. Stratton took the boy in his arms. Along with Philo Barnum, the Strattons and their son set out for the Franklin House, where Phineas T. Barnum waited.

CHAPTER TWO

The Prince of Humbugs

BEFORE A WARMING fire in the cozy parlor of the Franklin House, P. T. Barnum eagerly awaited the visit of Charley and his parents. He could not help but think the little Stratton boy could be a lucky break for him. By purchasing Scudder's American Museum and taking over the management of its many exhibitions and amusements, the balding and paunchy thirty-two-year-old Barnum had taken an important stride toward becoming America's premier entertainer. But he knew he needed fresh attractions to draw customers. Charles Stratton, Barnum thought to himself, could be a much-needed energizer.

Barnum's experiences in show business prepared him well for his meeting with Charley and his parents. Born in Bethel, Connecticut, on July 5, 1810, Barnum was not happy with shelling corn and riding plow horses on the

Thanks to his success with the American Museum and other even grander enterprises,
Phineas Taylor Barnum, pictured here in an engraving from his autobiography,
would come to be called America's Greatest Showman. ✦ *From* The Life of P. T. Barnum *(1855)*

family farm. He first saw New York as a boy of eleven when he helped drive a herd of cattle down to the city from Danbury, Connecticut. At sixteen, he moved to Brooklyn, New York, to take a job as a clerk in a grocery store. He was fascinated by the excitement of the city, but when his grandfather

Barnum's birthplace and childhood home in Bethel Village, a section of Danbury, Connecticut, where he was raised with five stepbrothers and stepsisters and, following his father's remarriage, five more siblings. ✦ *Bridgeport Public Library Historical Collection*

offered him the use of a carriage house rent-free in the center of Bethel, Barnum returned to Connecticut, where he married and started a family.

To earn a living, he opened a shop in the carriage house, selling fruit, candy, and fancy foods. Lotteries were extremely popular in those days, and Barnum set up an agency to sell tickets. He used some of his lottery profits to buy a printing press and started a four-page weekly newspaper called the *Herald of Freedom*.

Barnum was not only the paper's publisher, printer, and editor; he also assumed the role of columnist. He used the *Herald's* pages to express his opinions on a variety of subjects, including politics and religion. His views often got people angry, and on at least three occasions readers sued him for making false and malicious statements. One such suit, brought by a clergyman who felt his good name had been attacked, landed Barnum in jail. Using the pages of his newspaper to win sympathy for himself, Barnum was soon set free. On his release, he was hailed as a hero for his defense of the freedom of the press.

The episode was a valuable learning experience for Barnum. It showed him how the press could be used to influence public opinion. It was a lesson he would not forget.

At twenty-four, Barnum returned to New York with his wife and their young daughter. He managed a small boarding house and bought an interest in a grocery store. Neither business interested him very much. "I wanted," he said, "an opportunity where my faculties and energies could have full play."

In more specific terms, what Barnum was seeking was a chance for success in the entertainment business. "I had long fancied," Barnum said, "that I could succeed if I could only get hold of a public exhibition."

A public exhibition of his own. That was the thing.

At the time, public exhibitions were a popular form of entertainment. Few other choices existed. Decades would pass before the first primitive motion pictures became available. People were ready to pay to see something that would amuse, entertain, or even shock them.

Theaters and museums were the standard sources of entertainment. The latter often offered lecture rooms in which scientists would speak and sometimes exhibits would be available for viewing.

Freak shows were also popular. Human curiosities, as they were sometimes called, were first put on display in rented rooms or halls, and in museums too. Circuses and carnivals also exhibited freaks in minor or secondary attractions known as sideshows.

As revealed by newspaper advertisements and handbills of the time, these exhibits included Calvin Phillips ("The Famous American Dwarf Child"), "Young Indian Chiefs of the Onondaga Tribe," and Master Barber ("The Whiskered Child"), among others.

Chang and Eng Bunker, identical twins who were joined together through organs and skin, were the most famous curiosities of the time. From Siam (now

Thailand), they had come to the United States in 1829 and toured the nation until they had enough money to buy a plantation in North Carolina. Barnum put a wax figure of the twins on display in his museum. In 1860, they came out of retirement to appear in person for the showman.

Two-headed cows and three-horned sheep were billed by freak show promoters as cases of "science gone wrong." Some freak shows were outright hoaxes. For example, a very tall African American man from North Carolina, who appeared in chains and wore a primitive costume, was advertised as a "wild man." On stage, he would growl and snarl.

These freak show curiosities represented the type of public attraction that Barnum was seeking. He did not have to wait long to acquire one.

One July day in 1835, Barnum was at work in his store when an old friend from Connecticut dropped in for a visit. He brought Barnum news of an unusual public exhibit showing in Philadelphia that happened to be for sale. Barnum listened intently as his friend told him of the availability of Joice Heth, a blind, toothless, and partially paralyzed black slave said to be 161 years old. That was only part of the story. Heth also claimed to have been George Washington's nursemaid a century or so earlier.

Of all the "living curiosities" exhibited during the 1800s, none was more famous than conjoined twins Chang (right) and Eng (left). In 1838, after years on public display in Europe and the United States, they settled down on a plantation in North Carolina, married two sisters, and raised a large family.
♦ *University of North Carolina*

As his friend recited Joice Heth's story, Barnum could hardly believe his ears. This seemed to be the perfect opportunity for him. He booked passage on the next available stagecoach to Philadelphia. There he met the wrinkled and shriveled woman, who looked truly ancient. But when she spoke to audiences, her voice was strong and clear.

Barnum talked to the man who was exhibiting her. The man explained that Joice Heth was the property of a man who lived in Kentucky. Though slavery was illegal in the North, it was flourishing in the southern states, and Joice Heth had little say over her situation. The exhibitor kept the fact that she was still a slave quiet.

Barnum inspected what he was told was the original bill of sale for Heth. Dated February 5, 1727, it made Heth the property of George Washington's father. The man who owned her wanted three thousand dollars for "the possession of Joice Heth and the right of exhibiting her," but Barnum managed to talk him down to one thousand. Though technically this made Barnum a slave owner, he didn't think of it in this way. In his mind, he merely owned the rights to an exhibition.

By the fall of 1835, Barnum had sold his interest in the grocery store and was ready to launch his career as a showman. To make the public aware of his remarkable find, Barnum plastered New York with posters and flooded the city with handbills. He also laid siege to the city's many daily newspapers, providing them with a continual stream of colorful tales about Heth and her extraordinary life.

THE GREATEST
Natural & National
CURIOSITY
IN THE WORLD.

JOICE HETH.

Nurse to GEN. GEORGE WASHINGTON, (the Father of our Country,)
WILL BE SEEN AT

Barnum's Hotel, Bridgeport,

On FRIDAY, and SATURDAY, the 11th. & 12th days
of December, DAY and EVENING.

JOICE HETH is unquestionably the most astonishing and interesting curiosity in the
World! She was the slave of Augustine Washington, (the father of Gen. Washington,)
and was the first person who put clothes on the unconscious infant, who, in after days, led
our heroic fathers on to glory, to victory, and freedom. To use her own language when
speaking of the illustrious Father of his Country, "she raised him." JOICE HETH
was born in the year 1674, and has, consequently, now arrived at the astonishing

AGE OF 161 YEARS.

Pictured here as ancient and withered, with four-inch fingernails, Joice Heth was
described in such rousing terms by Barnum that many thousands of ticket buyers
flocked to see her. ✦ *newsbank.com*

That the story sounded mythical didn't seem to matter to him.

One of Barnum's advertisements claimed that Heth "was the slave of Augustine Washington (the father of George Washington), and was the first to put clothes on the unconscious infant." The same advertisement hailed Joice Heth as "unquestionably the most astonishing and interesting curiosity in the world."

The ad campaign paid rich dividends. The *New York Sun* called Joice Heth "a renowned relic" and declared, "[A] greater object of marvel and curiosity has never presented itself."

In August 1835, Barnum put "Auntie Joice"—his name for her—on public display at Niblo's Garden, a New York theater and concert hall. He presented her in dramatic fashion. Auntie Joice greeted the public while reclining on an elevated backless sofa in the center of a large room.

She proved to be a gallant performer. In her strong voice, the grizzled woman spoke of the first president as "dear little George" and proudly announced that she had been present at his birth. She often repeated this statement: "I raised him." She would also sing a few hymns and describe her baptism in the Potomac River in 1719.

Auntie Joice attracted huge numbers of people. She was Barnum's first big success.

Once her popularity began to fade in New York, Barnum took to the road with Auntie Joice. He exhibited her in Providence, Rhode Island; Boston; several smaller Massachusetts cities; and Hartford and New Haven in Connecticut. Everywhere, said Barnum, they met "with most satisfying success."

The Barnum-Heth partnership didn't last long. During the fall of 1835, Heth fell ill. Barnum sent her to be cared for at his brother Philo's home in Bethel, Connecticut. Her health continued to fail, and she died in February 1836. Barnum arranged for her to be interred in the village burial ground in Bethel.

Following her passing, a New York doctor requested permission to conduct a medical inspection of her body in the cause of science. The inspection revealed her age to be no more than eighty years, some eighty-one years less than Barnum had claimed. Barnum was denounced for staging a public hoax. The criticism stung. Barnum declared that he had bought the rights to exhibit Heth in "perfect good faith." He cited the bill of sale as evidence.

He said he had been led to believe that the father of George Washington had composed the document. It stated that Heth had been the "nurse of Washington." Barnum said that he now realized the document was a forgery. He claimed to have been tricked. Years later, however, Barnum admitted to a friend that he had always known the truth about Auntie Joice.

The uproar over Joice Heth earned Barnum a reputation for "humbug." He didn't seem to mind. In fact, he called himself "The Prince of Humbugs." Dictionaries define *humbug* as "something intended to delude or deceive; a trick or fraud." Barnum, however, assigned a different meaning to the term. Humbug, he

said, meant "putting on glittering appearances . . . to suddenly arrest public attention and attract the public eye and ear." Those who paid their money to look on Barnum's attractions did not always agree with his definition.

After the Joice Heth episode, Barnum made several attempts to establish himself as a showman by promoting variety acts that offered singing, dancing, and comedy. The shows flopped. In the spring of 1840, Mrs. Barnum gave birth to the couple's second daughter. The Barnums found themselves running out of money. Barnum, however, managed to remain optimistic. When it came to public attractions, he felt he had a special knowledge of what people wanted to see and would be willing to pay for.

When Scudder's American Museum became available, he jumped at the chance to acquire it. Housed in a sprawling five-story building the size of a department store, it offered a shabby assortment of shells, crystals, stuffed animals, and other knickknacks and curiosities. Barnum transformed Scudder's. After renaming it Barnum's American Museum, he hung huge banners and flags along the roof's edge and installed enormous paintings of giant snakes, bears, lions, and other animals in the museum's windows facing Broadway.

He strung American flags across Broadway, from the museum to a tree in front of St. Paul's Chapel, an honored site where George Washington had once worshiped. When members of the church congregation complained, Barnum accused them of being unpatriotic.

To attract attention to his museum, Barnum strung flags across Broadway, stretching from his building's roof to the trees in front of St. Paul's Chapel—much to the distress of church officials. ✦ *Bridgeport Public Library Historical Collection*

On the museum's roof, Barnum installed enough shrubbery to create a small park for strolling. The roof was also used to launch daily hot-air balloon rides.

Scudder's stuffed animals and artifact collections were cast aside in favor of a wide range of acts and what Barnum called "living curiosities" and "representatives of the wonderful." To showmen of the day, these were freaks—giants and dwarfs, the exceptionally fat or thin, and other human rarities. In the museum's spacious auditorium, the Lecture Room, Barnum offered oral presentations

by scientists, explorers, writers, and other specialists. Also presented in the Lecture Room was entertainment in the form of magicians, jugglers, ventriloquists, acrobats, "educated dogs," and a great array of singers and dancers.

Museum patrons were free to roam through the building, peering at the curiosities on exhibit, viewing the various acts, and attending lectures. With an admission of twenty-five cents, the museum was fairly priced.

One of the early exhibitions at the museum raised Barnum's reputation for humbuggery to new heights. It was an ugly, shriveled-up figure, about three

Barnum made good use of print advertising to publicize his museum. Other advertisers at the time rarely employed adjectives to describe what they were selling, but Barnum used them shamelessly. *Great* was one of his favorites.
 newsbank.com

feet in length, that had been sewn together from the body and tail of a big fish and the head, shoulders, and arms of a female baboon. He purchased the rights to exhibit the creature from a Boston museum owner. According to the contract, the object had been caught off the Fiji Islands in the South Pacific.

After he had dubbed the dried-up body "the Fejee Mermaid," Barnum began to "puff" her to the skies. He had ten thousand pamphlets printed and distributed to New Yorkers. He ordered an eight-foot-tall, full-color banner that depicted a beautiful creature soaring out of blue waters and had it hung above the museum's front entrance.

Barnum gave the many New York dailies special treatment. The newspapers of the day were dull in appearance, with column after column of national and local news. Illustrations were small in size and few in number. Barnum saw this as an opportunity. He called on the editors of several papers and provided each with an engraved block of wood—called a "cut"—that could be used to print a picture of the mermaid. He also furnished an elaborate description of the creature. Three newspapers used the illustrated story in their Sunday edition.

Barnum's efforts paid off. "Mermaid fever" gripped New York. Thousands of curious patrons crowded into the museum. Barnum had advertised the exhibition's duration as "one week only." But the response was so great that he stretched the Fejee Mermaid's run to a full month.

When interest in the exhibit began to fade, Barnum arranged for an uncle to

take the mermaid on a nationwide tour. All went well until the traveling exhibition reached Charleston, South Carolina. There the saga of the Fejee Mermaid came to an abrupt end. A local minister attacked the exhibit as a complete hoax. People were being defrauded, he said. He recognized that the creature consisted of a fishtail that had been attached to the upper body of a monkey. He shipped the mermaid back to Barnum, who returned what he referred to as the "lady fish" to its owner in Boston.

The Fejee Mermaid furor helped boost Barnum's reputation for humbuggery. Museum-goers came to expect it from him. Barnum once said that he occasionally met up with museum visitors who, in his words, "humbugged themselves." They were so wary of being tricked by the showman that they believed everything on exhibit to be a sham.

Barnum liked to tell the story of a white whale that he had purchased and put on exhibition after it had been captured off the coast of Labrador. Barnum had the whale placed in a fifty-foot-long tank, which he kept filled with salt water. A problem quickly developed. The whale was so frightened by the basement lighting system that it stayed on the bottom of the tank, thus concealing itself from visitors. But every couple of minutes or so, the whale was forced to hurry to the surface to blow out old air and breathe in fresh air.

One day a woman who had been watching the whale took Barnum aside

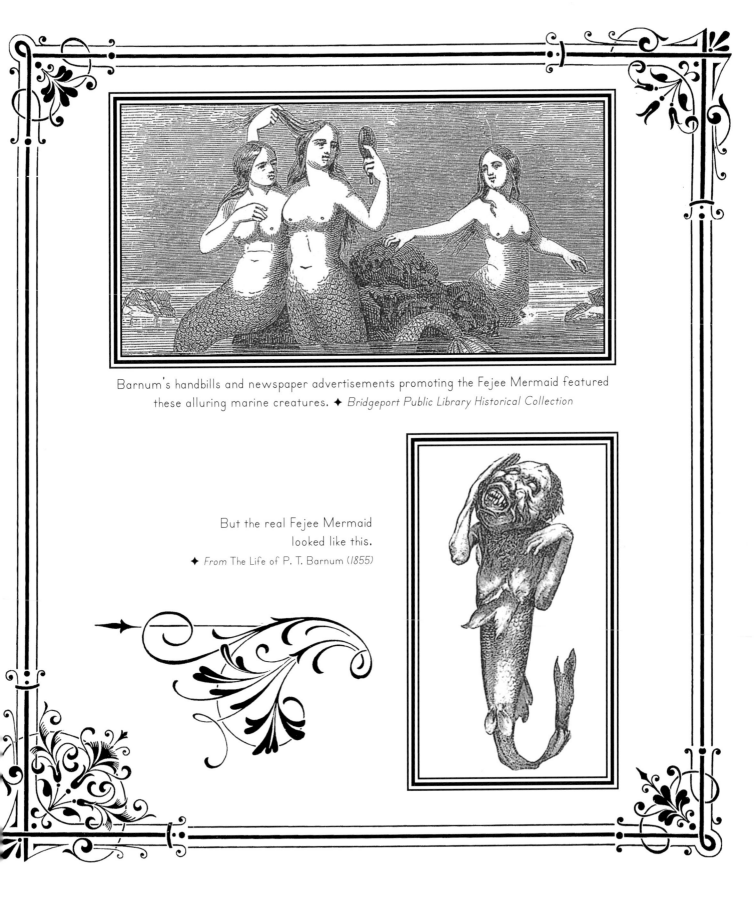

Barnum's handbills and newspaper advertisements promoting the Fejee Mermaid featured these alluring marine creatures. ✦ *Bridgeport Public Library Historical Collection*

But the real Fejee Mermaid looked like this.
✦ *From* The Life of P. T. Barnum *(1855)*

and congratulated him on the cleverness of the exhibit. She explained that she was convinced that the whale was made of rubber and artificially powered to rise to the surface after brief pauses on the bottom of the tank. Barnum realized the woman had humbugged herself. He knew it would be useless to try to convince her that the whale was real, and he simply complimented her on being the only person to discover the deception.

Barnum was fully aware that the Fejee Mermaid exhibit had been no harmless spoof. It was an outright deception. The public had been victimized.

Barnum now faced two problems. He needed a brand-new exhibit to draw patrons to his museum. He also needed to restore his reputation, darkly stained by Joice Heth and the Fejee Mermaid. He needed something real, something without a trace of fakery.

No wonder Barnum was anxious to meet Charley Stratton. What could be more real, more authentic, not to mention more appealing, than a perfectly proportioned miniature child? There was no doubt that the boy might help him recapture his good character.

When the Strattons and Barnum's brother entered the parlor of the Franklin House with Charley, Barnum took Charley into his arms and sat him on his knee. Barnum was immediately delighted with the young boy, describing him as "the smallest child I ever saw that could walk alone."

Charley surely realized how Barnum felt. Sitting on Barnum's lap in the warm parlor of the Franklin House, he looked up to see a wide smile on the showman's face.

As any four-year-old might be, Charley was very bashful. But, with coaxing, Barnum was able to get him to tell him his name. "Charles S. Stratton, son of Sherwood Stratton," the boy announced proudly.

"He was a bright-eyed little fellow," Barnum later said, "with light hair and ruddy cheeks, was perfectly healthy, and as symmetrical as an Apollo." Apollo was a major Greek god and the Greek ideal of manly beauty.

Barnum spoke with authority. He had a good deal of experience with people with dwarfism. He often exhibited dwarfs at his American Museum, and he knew there were many forms of dwarfism. Many of the dwarfs that Barnum had worked with had short arms and legs and relatively long upper bodies. Not Charley. He was, as Barnum noted, "symmetrical," perfectly proportioned. Barnum understood that Charley Stratton offered enormous possibilities. He felt that if the boy was presented properly, a great multitude of people would storm Barnum's museum to see him. He might even make the showman rich. Just as important, Charley could help blot the episodes involving Joice Heth and the Fejee Mermaid from the public's memory. Barnum was excited. Four-year-old Charley Stratton represented a new beginning.

○ ○ ○ DWARFS IN HISTORY ○ ○ ○

Barnum's public exhibition of Charley Stratton as General Tom Thumb was not something new. Dwarfs have performed and been displayed as curiosities since the earliest times. Representations of dwarfs can be found on Greek vases and in Egyptian art. The Greek philosopher Aristotle put dwarfs in the same category as young children and animals, saying they were inferior to persons of normal size. In ancient Egypt, dwarfs were often treated with respect, serving as nurses, animal keepers, jewelers, and entertainers in the residences of royalty. Some even achieved high positions within royal families.

During the fifteenth century, Queen Isabella I of Spain, who aided the voyages of Columbus, looked upon dwarfs as possessions to be treasured. When her brother Alfonso fell ill, she sent him her favorite dwarf as a gift. This famous 1631 painting by Diego Velázquez depicts Baltasar Carlos (right), the two-year-old heir to the Spanish throne, standing beside one of the several dwarfs who served as jesters and companions to the Spanish royal family.

In the United States, dwarfs were among the "human oddities" who were displayed at dime museums or toured with circus and carnival sideshows. There were several popular American dwarfs before Tom's time, including Major Stevens, the dwarf whom Mrs. Stratton's mother saw when she visited Barnum's museum.

○ ○ ○ ○ ○

Museum of Fine Arts, Boston

CHAPTER THREE

Makeover

HEN BARNUM ASKED Charley's parents about letting him exhibit their son, they differed in their responses. Mrs. Stratton scowled. "Show Charley with those freaks?" she said. Though she had agreed to the meeting with Barnum, she declared she would never permit him to display her son.

Mr. Stratton was more open to the proposition. He persuaded his wife to at least listen to what plans Mr. Barnum had for Charley.

Barnum explained that he wanted to hire Charley on an experimental basis, for only four weeks. He would pay the Strattons three dollars a week to exhibit their son, and, what's more, he promised to provide living quarters for Charley and his mother.

Mr. Stratton liked the idea of being paid three dollars a week. It was more than he was earning as a carpenter.

Mrs. Stratton found herself considering Barnum's proposal. She thought how nice it would be to go with Charley to New York City and be able to watch over him. And, after all, the arrangement was to last only four weeks. After that, they could come back to Bridgeport and their lives would return to normal.

It didn't take Barnum long to finalize the agreement. It was decided that Mrs. Stratton would bring Charley to New York early in December. After some preparation, he would begin performing at Barnum's Museum.

The railroad line from Bridgeport to New York had not yet been completed, so when the time came for Mrs. Stratton and Charley to leave home, they traveled to New York aboard the *Nimrod*, a steam-powered vessel. After making its way through Long Island Sound to the East River on Manhattan's eastern fringe, the *Nimrod* landed its passengers at a pier in Lower Manhattan, and Mrs. Stratton hailed a horse-drawn cab to take them to Barnum's Museum. As she and Charley alighted from the vehicle, a young boy thrust a printed notice into her hand. It read:

P. T. Barnum of the American Museum, Broadway at Ann Street, is proud to announce that he has imported from London to add to his collection of extraordinary curiosities from all over the world, the rarest, the tiniest, the most diminutive dwarf imaginable—TOM THUMB, ELEVEN YEARS OLD AND ONLY TWENTY-FIVE INCHES HIGH, JUST ARRIVED FROM ENGLAND!!!

The Strattons had been humbugged.

Mrs. Stratton was furious. With Charley in her arms, she rushed into the museum in a rage and burst into Barnum's office. Standing before the bewildered showman's desk, she demanded to know why Charley had been described as being eleven years old and "just arrived from England."

Barnum smiled and remained calm. He spoke in a soothing voice. He admitted that the announcement "contained two deceptions," but he said he felt justified in making them.

In regards to Charley's age, Barnum explained that if he had said that Charley was only five years old, people might not believe that he was a dwarf. They would think he was a small five-year-old. "It would have been impossible to excite the interest or awaken the curiosity of the public," Barnum said. By identifying him as a boy of eleven, people would be more likely to believe that he was a dwarf and be impressed by the extent of his dwarfism.

Barnum went on to explain that promoting the idea that Charley was foreign-born was important too. It would lead people to believe that Barnum had gone to great expense to bring Charley to America. Besides, Americans had "a fancy for European exotics," Barnum said.

Broadway, the street address of Barnum's American Museum, was full of life. Visitors flocked to its fashionable stores, fine hotels, and, of course, the museum itself. ✦ *New York Public Library*

Barnum next explained why he chose the name Tom Thumb for Charley. Becoming very earnest, he told Mrs. Stratton that the public would not likely pay to see a young boy named Charles Sherwood Stratton. But Tom Thumb was a different matter.

Barnum had plucked the name from English folklore. Tom Thumb had appeared in a book by Henry Fielding, titled *The Tragedy of Tragedies; or, the History of Tom Thumb the Great,* published in 1731. A young boy no bigger than his father's thumb, Tom is both clumsy and mischievous. In one episode, he falls into the batter for a cake that his mother is preparing. When the cake, with Tom inside, is baked and begins to move, Tom's mother believes it to be enchanted.

In the years that followed the publication of Fielding's book, other versions of the Tom Thumb story appeared.

Barnum didn't much care about the history of the name. All he knew was that it was familiar and he liked it. "Tom Thumb" fit

Folktales and legends about Tom Thumb, a child no bigger than his father's thumb (and easy prey for a ravenous bird), go back to the 1600s, and thumb-size characters are found in the literature of many cultures.
✦ *New York Public Library*

Charley perfectly. It was an otherworldly name. It would increase Charley's appeal by arousing curiosity.

Later, Barnum added the title General to the name as another way of increasing the boy's prestige but also for a touch of humor. The practice of assigning titles was common among exhibits that featured people with dwarfism. Princess, Admiral, Count, and Commodore were other designations that were pinned on freak show dwarfs. Labels like these were a way of poking fun at the object of the title, something like calling a very tall person Shorty.

In the days before Charley and his mother arrived, Barnum had carefully planned how the little boy would be presented. He realized that Charley was a remarkable find. He was bright and attractive. He could be a star. Barnum resolved to make the most of the boy's talents.

The showman had no intention of thrusting Charley or any of his performers onto the stage just so audiences could stare and gawk at them. That was not Barnum's way. To enhance their appeal, some of his performers were schooled to perform acrobatic feats that appeared well beyond their skill levels. An armless man, a regular at Barnum's museum, cut paper valentines and shot a bow and arrow with his feet. Another of Barnum's armless performers wrote quite legibly by holding a pen between his toes.

Many of the people that Barnum exhibited were taught to dance, sing, play a musical instrument, or recite a poem or piece of prose. Barnum planned to

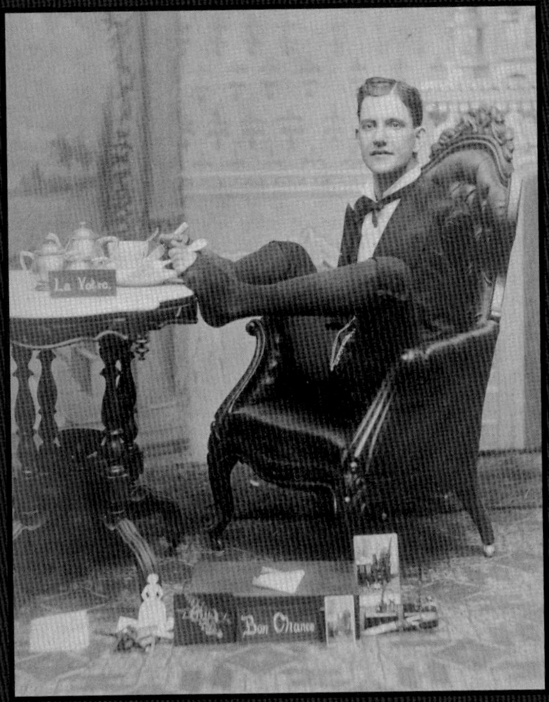
La Votre.
Bon Chance

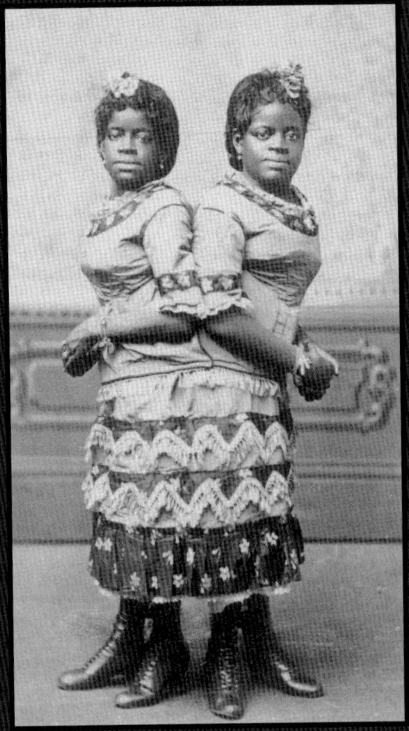

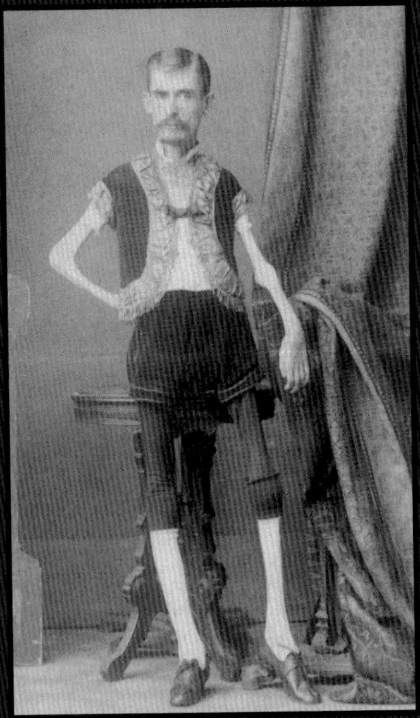

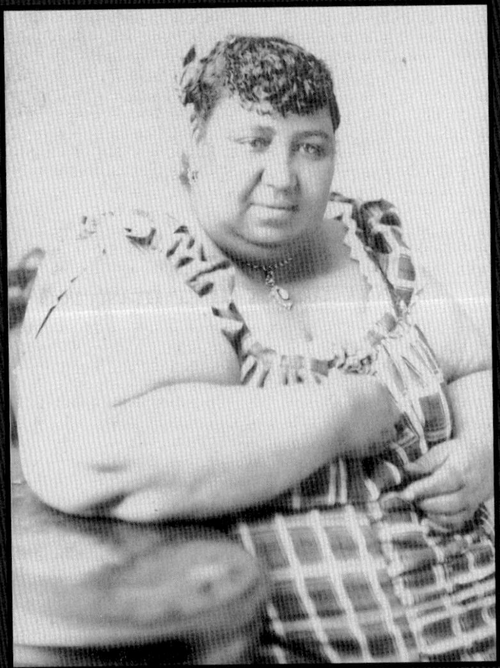

present Charley as a well-mannered, well-educated young man, not as a child. But Barnum fully realized that Charley's natural talents as a performer could be used to great advantage.

When Charley and his mother arrived in New York, Barnum arranged for them to live on the fifth floor of the museum. Two giants lived across the hall. Barnum and his family, which now included three daughters, lived next to the museum in a building that had once been a billiard parlor.

Charley and his mother had hardly gotten settled in their new quarters when the boy's training began. Whenever Barnum could steal an hour or so from his obligations at the museum, he would act as Charley's teacher. He first instructed him in good manners, telling him that it was important to get into the habit of saying "please" and "thank you." When Charley addressed an adult, Barnum wanted him to use the word "sir" or "ma'am." Barnum also tutored Charley in the proper use of the knife and fork and other matters of table etiquette.

Once Charley had mastered this phase of his training, Barnum began introducing him to the various roles he would play when he began to perform on

Among the men and women advertised and exhibited as "human curiosities and oddities" during the mid to late 1800s were Charles Tripp, "The Armless Wonder," who could manipulate cutlery with his toes; Millie and Christine McCoy, conjoined twins born in slavery; Mr. I. W. Sprague, "The Human Skeleton," who weighed just forty-three pounds; and an unidentified "fat lady."
✦ *Special Collections Research Center, Syracuse University Library*

To prepare Charley for his stage debut, Barnum spent days teaching the young boy
songs, poems, and a few dance steps, as well as how to imitate several
famous individuals. ✦ *From* The Life of P. T. Barnum *(1855)*

stage. To go with each role, Barnum ordered an appropriate costume for Charley
and had him memorize a number of witty remarks.

Barnum ordered clothes for Charley that were of the highest quality and
produced by the finest tailors. His boots were made of the softest leather.
Of Charley's gloves, Barnum said, "Nothing so small or fairy-like were before

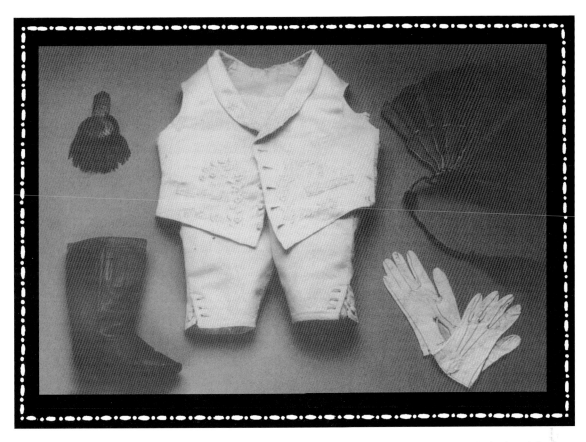

A sampling of the fine clothing and accessories Barnum had arranged to be made by hand for Charley. ✦ *Bridgeport History Center, Bridgeport Public Library Corbit Collection*

manufactured." Barnum also provided Charley with several canes, each of which was no more than ten or twelve inches in length.

Barnum could not help but be impressed by Charley. Not only was the boy enthusiastic about learning, but he also quickly memorized the lines he was to deliver on stage. He showed a natural gift for mimicry—for playfully imitating the mannerisms of the characters he was to depict. He took great pleasure in saluting, clicking his heels, twirling his cane, and strutting about the stage.

Barnum later noted that after several weeks of training sessions, a bond developed between them. "He became very fond of me," said Barnum. "I was, and still am, similarly attached to him."

Charley was enjoying himself, which was fortunate, for he had no choice in the matter. He was, after all, barely five years old. He did what his parents and Barnum wanted him to do. By joining the cast at Barnum's Museum, Charley was being assigned an occupation from which he would never break loose. And he would be known as Tom Thumb for the rest of his life.

Of all the characters that Tom portrayed, Napoleon Bonaparte was his favorite. It was a role he would play off and on for the rest of his life. ✦ *Bridgeport Public Library Historical Collection*

CHAPTER FOUR

On Stage

NCE TOM and his mother were settled in their new living quarters, Barnum invited them on a tour of the museum. They were fascinated by what they saw. There were giants, dwarfs, and fat ladies on exhibit, of course, as well as jugglers and ventriloquists, but also rope dancers, educated dogs, and trained fleas. They watched glass-blowing displays, knitting machines in operation, and demonstrations of an unusual gold-plating contraption.

Barnum's most noted dwarf at the time was Major Stevens, whom he billed as "The American Dwarf." Forty years old and pudgy, Major Stevens was thirty-seven inches in height, a foot taller than Tom. The major was stunned and bewildered when he saw Tom for the first time. "I may be billed hereafter, perhaps, as a giant," he said.

Major Stevens voiced uncertainty as to where his career might be headed to now that Tom was on the scene. He was right to be worried. Soon after Tom showed up, he was out of a job.

It didn't take Tom long to understand that as a dwarf like Major Stevens, he was regarded as a "born freak" by the museum people. Giants and individuals with physical abnormalities also fell into that category.

There were also "made freaks." These men and women were unique because they had developed some unusual skill. Made freaks included sword swallowers, fire eaters, and performers with special talents, such as the ability to lie on a bed of nails or walk up and down a ladder with sharp swords for rungs. Barnum once employed a made freak who could make music with his nostrils.

When Barnum purchased the museum, it was known for its collection of stuffed animals, mostly birds and small animals such as raccoons and beavers. Barnum added bigger animal specimens to the collection, including zebras, lions, grizzly bears, and an elephant.

Barnum's museum staff included a taxidermist, a specialist in preparing, preserving, and stuffing the skins of animals. Barnum encouraged museum visitors to bring their recently deceased pets to have them stuffed and mounted—for a fee, of course.

Miss Trixie Richardson, the tattooed woman, was a "made freak"—she altered her body by covering its surface with tattoos. Other made freaks developed special skills, such as fire eating. ✦ *Special Collections Research Center, Syracuse University Library*

Miss Trixie
Richardson

Tatooed by
Chas. Wagner, N.Y.

From the beginning, Barnum's ambition was to acquire and exhibit an assortment of live exotic animals. Because he was short of funds at the time, he could purchase only small, commonplace creatures. Starting with snakes, he quickly built an impressive reptile collection. Growing up in Connecticut, Tom had seen only harmless garter snakes and such, and he was delighted to view the more unusual examples that Barnum offered. Some were as fearsome as any jungle beast. Much later, in a press release of the 1850s, Barnum described one of the snakes as capable of eating "a good sized dog" and another was said to have "devoured a woman and child before it was taken."

Barnum's collection of live exotic animals eventually included an orangutan, a royal Bengal tiger, a leopard, a grizzly bear, and a den of lions. He would send expeditions to the far corners of the earth to stock his menagerie.

At the time Tom began performing for Barnum, the showman was in the midst of enlarging and modernizing the museum's theater, the Lecture Room. It eventually was furnished with a huge balcony, elegant box seats, and crystal chandeliers, and could seat three thousand people. The Lecture Room was not only noteworthy for its size. It also represented an important cultural advance. In the first half of the nineteenth century, New York theaters had a bad reputation. Rowdiness and drunkenness were common among audiences. No

Anna Swan, seven feet tall, and her husband, Martin van Buren Bates, were "born freaks."
Like Tom, they were born into their condition. To accentuate their height, the couple often posed
with a person of average size. ✦ *Special Collections Research Center, Syracuse University Library*

respectable person would go to the theater. But Barnum hired plainclothes detectives to patrol the Lecture Room. They were under orders to eject "every person of either sex whose actions indicated loose habits." Barnum's Lecture Room became a place of family entertainment where men, women, and even children could be amused and educated.

Tom made his debut on the Lecture Room's stage on December 9, 1842. He was not quite five years old.

The huge Lecture Room of the American Museum, where Tom appeared regularly, was one of the finest musical theaters in the country in the mid-1800s. ✦ *New York Public Library*

Barnum stepped to the front of the stage to introduce his latest find. "Ladies and Gentlemen," the theater manager loudly announced, "P. T. Barnum presents to you General Tom Thumb. He is the rarest, the most incredible, the smallest specimen of humanity that has ever visited the earth . . . a young Englishman, eleven years old, only two feet high, weighing but fifteen pounds that I imported for your pleasure from London."

With that, Tom hurried out onto the stage, saluted the audience, and strutted about while holding high his cane. Mounting a raised platform at the center of the stage, Tom sang "Yankee Doodle" in his high-pitched voice.

> *Yankee Doodle went to town,*
> *Riding on a pony,*
> *Stuck a feather in his cap*
> *And called it macaroni.*
> *Yankee Doodle, keep it up,*
> *Yankee Doodle dandy.*
> *Mind the music and the step*
> *And with the girls be handy.*

A song that dated to the 1750s, "Yankee Doodle" is thought to have been sung by British soldiers to poke fun at the bedraggled, poorly organized "Yankees" (Americans), whom they fought alongside during the French and Indian

War. Whenever Tom sang the song, adding several of its more than one hundred verses, he always drew applause and cheers. The song came to be identified with him throughout his career.

It didn't take Tom long to become skilled and confident on stage. He developed a routine in which he would stand at the front of the stage and relate some personal history and answer questions from audience members. Barnum sometimes used "plants," people placed secretly in the audience who asked Tom questions from a memorized script. Tom would be ready with joking answers.

In the first years of his stage career in New York and elsewhere, Tom usually appeared with an actor who served as his comedy partner, playing the role of "Doctor." At first, Barnum himself often played the part.

Here is the text of one of their scripts:

DOCTOR: It is only by placing the General in contrast with a very small child that the audience can form the right conception of his real height. Will some little boy step up on the stage for a moment?

TOM: I would rather have a little miss.

DOCTOR: A little miss? Well, I don't know why you shouldn't be satisfied with a little boy. Will you pick one yourself?

TOM: Yes, sir. Will some little miss come and take a seat upon my sofa?

DOCTOR: Will somebody have the kindness to allow a little miss between the ages of five and ten to come up on the stage and show the contrast between the two?

TOM: You needn't be afraid.

[A little girl went up on the stage.]

DOCTOR: This little miss is __ years of age and the General is eleven. The audience will perceive the contrast at once. It is often remarked that when the General is placed upon the stage alone that he appears much larger than he is by at least a head, but when placed alongside of a child the audience can judge exactly of his size. Now, sir, will you be kind enough to place the little miss by your side.

[Tom seated himself next to the little girl.]

DOCTOR: Well, General, how do you progress with your courtship?

TOM: First rate, sir.

DOCTOR: Is the little miss any wise bashful?

TOM: A little, sir.

DOCTOR: Well, you must endeavor to encourage her as well as you can.

[Tom kissed the little girl.]

The audience would then cheer and applaud.

Tom soon became aware that it was not only the little girls who were drawn to him. Older women were too. They thought he was "cute." They wanted to touch him, hug him, and kiss him.

He learned to take advantage of his appeal. Not only did he sell kisses, but he also began to offer a booklet about himself for twenty-five cents. It told Barnum's version of Tom's life story and provided the lyrics to some of the songs that Tom sang. The little booklet was undoubtedly Barnum's creation.

Its availability was played up in this popular exchange between Tom, who would be dressed as a Scottish Highlander, a soldier of a Highland regiment, and his onstage partner:

DOCTOR: What dress is this, General?

TOM: It's my Highland costume.

DOCTOR: What is that in your hand, General?

TOM: My claymore. [A double-edged sword.]

DOCTOR: To what use do you put it to?

TOM: I fight with it.

DOCTOR: Fight! I'd like to know if you've ever been in battle.

TOM: How could I be a general if I have never been in battle?

DOCTOR: Why, sir, I know several generals who have never smelt gunpowder . . .Will you favor the audience with a Scotch song?

TOM: Yes, sir. [Tom then sang "Come Sit Thee Down," a Scottish ballad.]

DOCTOR: Now, General, will you be kind enough to astonish the audience by dancing the Highland fling?

TOM: Yes, sir. [Tom then offered his version of the lively Scottish dance, traditionally performed by soldiers following a victory.]

DOCTOR: I will here state the General has an interesting book containing an account of his life and travels and also a lithographic portrait which the audience can procure in the room below at the conclusion of the performance. What do you charge for them, General?

TOM: A stamped receipt.

DOCTOR: And what is a "stamped receipt"?

TOM: A kiss.

In what became a popular windup to his act, Tom would put on an elastic body stocking. He would then pose in a series of "Grecian statues." The subjects included Romulus, who, with his twin brother Remus, was one of the mythic founders of the city of Rome; Samson, a biblical warrior of great strength; and Cain, another biblical figure, the first son of Adam and Eve. *Ooohs* and *aaahs* from the audience greeted each pose.

Tom gave two shows a day in the Lecture Room. When he was not performing, he often spent time rehearsing a new song or dance. When the weather was agreeable, his mother would take him on walks, often to City Hall Park, just north of the museum. Tom especially liked going down to the docks along the East River to see the scores of huge sailing ships moored there.

When Barnum found the time, he would read to Tom from storybooks. These sessions were a great joy to Tom. They also were a new experience. Tom's mother, having little education, had never learned to read and was not able to share books with her son.

Although Tom was not an overnight success, his popularity grew quickly, despite competition from the usual attractions at the museum. He was all Barnum had hoped for and more. At the end of the first month, Barnum drew up a contract that raised Tom's salary to seven dollars a week. Of that amount, three dollars went to Tom's father, who had joined Mrs. Stratton and was now doing odd jobs

GENERAL TOM THUMB

CITIZEN

COURT DRESS

HIGHLAND

for the museum. Barnum also paid a fifty-dollar bonus to Tom and his family before the year ended.

The following year, as Tom's ability to draw customers continued to shoot up, Barnum increased his weekly salary to twenty-five dollars, "and he fairly earned it," the showman said. By today's standards, Tom's weekly earnings would have amounted to several hundred dollars.

Tom loved being a stage performer. He also enjoyed the money he was receiving. He didn't like spending it, however. Tom hoarded every cent he earned and felt quite self-satisfied as his savings kept growing.

In His Different Characters

NAPOLEON   VILLIKINS   OUR MARY ANN

CAIN   SAILOR   ROMULUS

In picking out characters for Tom to play on stage, Barnum turned to a wide range of
sources. Cain was a biblical figure who murdered his brother, Abel; Romulus, according to ancient
legend, was the first king of Rome; the fictional Villikins was a rich London merchant
portrayed in an English folk song. Portraying the character "Our Mary Ann"—the nickname of
Mary Ann Lee, who headed an American ballet company in the 1840s—gave Tom the chance to
appear in women's dress. ✦ *Bridgeport Public Library Historical Collection*

Tom's success made for an enormous improvement in Barnum's state of af-
fairs. Barnum was able to make the final payment on the loan he had taken out
to buy the American Museum. He also was able to purchase Peale's Museum, his
chief rival in New York City. Barnum was now the only show in town.

Although his business was thriving, Barnum kept a close eye on attendance
figures. At the first sign that interest in Tom was beginning to wane, he would
arrange for him to present his act in other cities, and he would introduce a fresh
attraction in New York.

Tom's mother always traveled with him on the tours. She saw to it that Tom ate and slept properly. She also looked after the costumes he wore, washing and ironing them and mending anything that got damaged. Tom's father went along, too. At Tom's performances, he worked as the ticket taker. Tom's sisters remained in Bridgeport, cared for by Mrs. Fairchild.

Barnum stayed in New York when Tom went on the road. In his place, he sent Fordyce Hitchcock, a lifelong friend, as the director of the tour. Tom also traveled with a tutor, who instructed him in reading, writing, and arithmetic, and other school subjects. The tutor, along with a dancing master, also devised new roles for Tom to play.

Tom appeared for six weeks at the Boston Museum, where he attracted enormous crowds. He enjoyed it all, shaking hands and kissing the ladies, which, as one eyewitness observed, it was "impossible to prevent his doing."

After Boston, Barnum arranged for Tom to appear in theaters in Charleston, South Carolina, and in Philadelphia and Baltimore. The *Baltimore Sun* said of Tom: "Were he deformed or sickly, we might pity him; but he is so manly, so handsome, so hearty and happy, that we look at him as being from some other sphere."

Tom seemed to thrive on all that was taking place. As a small child in Bridgeport, he had always had an impish nature. He was often playfully naughty with his mother and family friends. Mischief was part of his personality. On stage at

Barnum's, when appearing as Napoleon or a soldier, he was, in a sense, playing a prank on the audience. He laughed at what he was doing. The audience laughed with him, not at him. Tom loved it.

Meanwhile, Barnum was making plans for the future. Having triumphed in America, the showman turned his eyes toward Europe. "Young man," he said to Tom one day, "what would you think of our going to England to say hello to the queen?"

Before Tom had a chance to answer, his mother broke in. "You don't mean Queen Victoria?" she asked excitedly.

"I do, Mrs. Stratton," said Barnum. "Victoria must be dying to see our little wonder."

Then Barnum told them that he was planning a European tour for Tom and inviting Tom's mother and father to go along. "So we're sailing for England in January," he declared.

Late in December 1843 and early in January 1844, Barnum placed advertisements in New York newspapers announcing Tom's departure for London. They were meant to make people aware that they had only a few more chances to see Tom. Barnum's ploy worked. "On one day," the *New York Tribune* reported, "General Tom Thumb received 15,000 visitors." It seemed all of New York wanted to see Tom Thumb.

In his final days on the Lecture Room stage, Tom performed with even more

than his usual enthusiasm. Not only was he tickled by the overflow crowds and their resounding cheers and applause, but he was energized by the idea that the biggest adventure of his young life was about to begin.

CHAPTER FIVE

Command Performance

TRUMPETS BLARED. Trombones bellowed. Bass drums boomed.

The official New York City Brass Band paraded down Broadway shortly before noon on January 18, 1844, playing "Yankee Doodle," Tom's theme song. Just past city hall, the marchers turned onto Fulton Street and headed for the East River pier, where the packet *Yorkshire* waited.

Tom was so excited, he hardly noticed the winter cold. Bundled in a neatly tailored overcoat, he stood on the driver's seat of the splendid horse-drawn four-wheeled carriage that followed the band, waving to the crowds lining both sides of the street. His face was red. His dark eyes gleamed.

Tom's mother and father rode inside the carriage and peered out at the crowd.

They looked worried, as if fearful that the raucous mob might overrun their vehicle.

At the pier, thousands of people greeted the carriage with thunderous cheers. When the throng surged around the carriage, Tom's father acted quickly. He took his son in his arms and squeezed through the mob to the safe haven offered by the ship. Once on board, Tom and his parents stood at the rail and waved handkerchiefs to the cheering spectators.

"Yes, I'm returning General Tom Thumb to England at the request of Queen Victoria," Barnum announced to newspaper reporters. "Now that I've made the little Englishman famous, Her Majesty wishes to see him."

The three-masted, square-rigged *Yorkshire* was one of the fastest packets then in service. The packets were a class of about fifty vessels that made regular sailings between New York and Liverpool, England, during the 1840s. Carrying freight, mail, and passengers, they were the fastest means of communication between the United States and Europe.

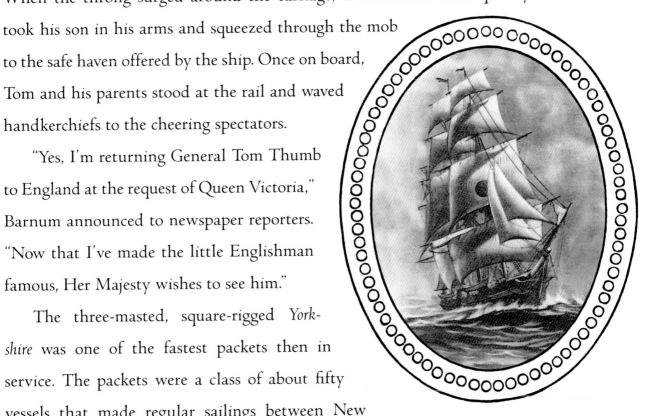

The U.S. Postal Service featured the *Yorkshire* in this commemorative postcard issued in 1988.
♦ *U.S. Postal Service*

The *Yorkshire* had made an Atlantic crossing in fifteen and a half days, considered an "incredible" feat. Only 167 feet in length, the ship carried fourteen passengers, who traveled in luxury. Tom and his mother occupied a large, handsomely furnished stateroom. His father had a stateroom of his own. They could relax in the ship's luxurious salon, with its red plush chairs and sofas, glittering crystal chandeliers, and mirrored walls.

Thanks to the two cows on the ship, Tom had fresh milk and the adults had cream for their coffee. There were live chickens, ducks, pigs, and sheep on board as well, so the meat for meals was fresh too.

The ship had hardly left New York when Tom's mother got seasick. She was forced to spend the early days of the voyage in her stateroom berth. Tom therefore had more than his usual amount of freedom.

Passengers often spotted him striding happily about the open deck. He sometimes puffed on a cigar, which seemed unusually large in his tiny fingers. He greeted one and all with a friendly "Hi, ya."

Tom became a favorite of the ship's crew. They showed him how to perform the hornpipe, a lively jiglike dance. And they taught him to sing "Life on the Ocean Wave." On calm evenings, he sometimes serenaded passengers with the song:

> *Oh, for the life on the ocean wave,*
> *A home on the rolling deep,*
> *Where the scattered waters rave,*

And the winds their revels keep.

Because of unfavorable winds, it took the *Yorkshire* nineteen days to complete the Atlantic crossing. At the Liverpool dock, thousands of people had assembled to greet the ship, most of them hoping to get a look at Tom as he stepped off board. But Barnum, as ever, was shrewd. The showman had no wish to allow anyone to get even a glimpse of Tom without paying for the privilege. He convinced Mrs. Stratton to bundle Tom in a blanket and carry him, like an infant, from the ship. Hardly anyone noticed when Mrs. Stratton left the *Yorkshire* with her son cradled in her arms.

Arranging for Tom to meet Queen Victoria of England was now Barnum's chief mission. He knew that if he could manage to get an audience for Tom with the queen, and she enjoyed his company, he would become an overnight celebrity. Everyone in England would then want to see him. Barnum also knew that achieving that goal would not be easy.

Despite what he had told the press and Mrs. Stratton, Barnum knew it was likely that the queen had never heard of Tom. And even if she did know his name, there was no reason for her to look upon him as special in any way. Dwarfs were frequently put on public display in England in what were called "penny shows."

Furthermore, Barnum had never been to England. And he had no friends he could turn to for help or introductions.

Barnum understood that to get an invitation to Buckingham Palace, the queen's residence, he had to create tremendous interest in Tom, so much interest that the queen would become curious and express a desire to see him.

Barnum began his campaign by exhibiting Tom in a Liverpool theater for a few nights. This was mainly to let the public know that Tom had arrived in England. Despite their eagerness to get a free glimpse of Tom upon his arrival, the people of Liverpool had little interest in paying to see him, even though Barnum advertised Tom as the "SMALLEST PERSON THAT EVER WALKED THE EARTH." He played mostly to empty seats.

Barnum decided to move operations to London. His goal remained the same: to attract the attention of the queen. He began by renting a furnished mansion in one of the city's most fashionable districts. To staff his household, he hired an array of servants, including a valet, a butler, a chef, and several liverymen to care for the horses and carriages.

Once he had his manor house running smoothly, Barnum sent out invitations to wealthy and influential Londoners, inviting them to his home to meet privately with Tom. The invitations were tastefully engraved, addressed artfully by hand, and delivered by messenger.

Most of the invited guests were happy to come. Tom was in top form. He greeted each visitor with bows and flattery. "How d'ya do," he said, putting out his little hand.

Barnum established his headquarters in an elegant mansion in the West End, which was fast becoming one of London's most fashionable areas. It was not far from Charing Cross, pictured in this engraving. ✦ *Prints & Photographs Division, New York Public Library*

One day, the mail brought Barnum just the kind of invitation he desired. It was from Baroness Rothschild, the wife of Baron Lionel Rothschild, one of the richest bankers in the world.

"Dear Mr. Barnum," the invitation began. "I am giving a private party at my home. Would it be asking too much of you to bring your wonderful Tom Thumb to entertain my guests? I will send a carriage for you."

In this engraving made in England in 1844, the artist
surrounded Tom with several commonplace objects to
help define his size. ✦ *New York Public Library*

On the appointed evening, the Rothschilds' elegant carriage transported Barnum and Tom through the streets of London and up the driveway to the mansion. At the door, half a dozen servants dressed in black coats and pantaloons, with white vests, gloves, and scarves, greeted the two.

Barnum and Tom were escorted up a broad flight of marble stairs to the drawing room. There the baroness and some twenty lords and ladies waited.

Tom took it all in stride. He felt as he had back at the Sterling House in Bridgeport, where he was the center of attention, entertaining the cooks and waitresses. He pranced out, grinned and waved, and bowed low from the waist. "Good evening, Ladies and Gentlemen," he called out. Much of his humor that night was based on puns, words that have two different meanings or different words that sound alike. "I am only a *Thumb*," he said, "but a good *hand* in a *general* way of amusing you." He also noted, "Though I am a *mite*, I am *mighty*."

Barnum and Tom spent two hours at the Rothschilds' home. As they were leaving, a purse filled with gold coins was pressed into Barnum's hand, a token of gratitude for providing an evening of entertainment. Barnum caressed the bulging purse and smiled to himself.

Barnum's next move was to present Tom at London's Egyptian Hall, a popular theater and entertainment center. Now that many members of London's aristocracy were familiar with Tom, his show was a great success. Every performance was a sellout, with lords and ladies snatching up the best seats.

But Barnum's goal was still to secure an audience for Tom with Queen Victoria. He felt certain it would help make him a favorite of the British public. However, as the days passed with no word from the royal family, his hopes began to fade.

Then Barnum's luck changed. One morning, at a breakfast arranged by Edward Everett, a noted statesman and orator from Massachusetts who was then serving as the American minister to England, Barnum met Charles Murray, another guest, who held the office of master of the queen's household.

Murray was curious about Tom. "Is he really only twenty-five inches high?" he asked.

"Yes," said Barnum. "He is twelve years old and weighs fifteen pounds. Too bad the queen didn't see him."

Murray's brow wrinkled.

Barnum, aware of the rivalry between the English and French thrones, then played his trump card. He went on to explain that he and Tom were planning to leave England shortly for France. There Tom was to meet Louis Philippe, the French king.

Now Murray seemed truly troubled. It would be unthinkable for the French monarch to meet Tom before the queen did. Murray wouldn't permit it.

The very next morning an officer of the Queen's Life Guard turned up at

Barnum's residence with an invitation from the queen. It requested that General Tom Thumb and his guardian, Phineas Taylor Barnum, appear at Buckingham Palace, the official residence of the queen, on March 23, 1844. Barnum had triumphed.

When they arrived at the palace on the given day, a lord-in-waiting instructed Barnum and Tom on how to act in their audience with the queen. They were told not to speak to her directly. Should Her Majesty ask a question, they were to reply to the lord-in-waiting, not to the queen herself. And when it came time for them to leave the queen's presence, they were to back out of the room, to remain facing the queen as they departed.

Barnum and Tom were led up a long flight of marble stairs and then down a red-carpeted corridor to the queen's picture gallery. When the doors were thrown open and they stepped into the room, they heard the booming voice of an attendant announce: "Phineas T. Barnum! General Tom Thumb!"

Victoria, who was twenty-four years old, had become queen seven years before. She stood at the far end of the room, a rather plain-looking young woman wearing a simple black dress and no jewelry. She was smiling. She was surrounded by about twenty members of the nobility, among them, her husband, Prince Albert, and the Duchess of Kent.

Tossing aside all the rules of court etiquette he had just been briefed on, Tom

In 1844, when Tom first met Great Britain's
Queen Victoria, she was twenty-four years old
and had reigned for seven years.
She would continue as queen until 1901,
the year of her death. ✦ *New York Public Library*

took a few steps forward, then bowed grace-
fully and exclaimed, "Good evening,
Ladies and Gentlemen!"

Barnum gasped, fearful as
to how the queen might re-
act to Tom's boldness. But
a loud burst of laughter
from the group stilled
his worries.

The queen came for-
ward, took Tom by the
hand, and began leading
him through the gallery,
pointing out various works
of art. Tom looked up at each
and seemed interested. He told
the queen that her picture gallery
was "first rate."

Before the tour ended, Tom
asked the queen whether he might
see the Prince of Wales. Tom was

referring to Bertie, the queen's two-and-a-half-year-old son. The queen replied that Bertie was in bed asleep but that Tom would be able to meet him on some future visit.

Tom then performed for the group, singing, dancing, doing imitations, and reciting sketches. The queen, her husband, and all the lords and ladies responded with more laughter and applause than they had produced in a long time.

When it came time to leave, Barnum began backing out of the long gallery, as he had been instructed to do. Tom did the same. But since Tom was unable to keep up with the fast pace set by Barnum, he had to turn and run for several steps in order to catch up with him. He had to repeat this sequence several times. The royal spectators roared with delight.

The queen's pet dog, a small poodle, unaccustomed to such excitement, began barking. The dog rushed forward and snapped at Tom's feet. For someone of Tom's size, the animal was a real threat. But Tom was equal to the occasion. Using the little cane he was carrying as a sword, he launched a playful mock attack upon the poodle. The lords and ladies again filled the gallery with their laughter.

After the excitement, Barnum and Tom were served refreshments and taken on a tour of the palace.

Although Tom's performance brought much applause and laughter, the queen had serious thoughts about the evening. Before she retired, Victoria took out her

Caught off-guard when Queen Victoria's pet poodle started barking, Tom, armed with a tiny wooden cane, launched a mock attack on the animal. ✦ *From* The Life of P. T. Barnum *(1855)*

diary and wrote: "After dinner, we saw the greatest curiosity I, or indeed anybody ever saw—a little dwarf, only 25 inches high & 15 pounds in weight. He made the funniest little bow, putting out his hand & saying, 'much obliged Mam.' One cannot help feeling sorry for the poor little thing & wishing he could be properly cared for, for the people that show him off tease him a great deal, I should think."

In her diary entry, the queen also noted that Tom "was born in [18]32, which makes him 12 years old." Of course, Tom was still only six.

Queen Victoria had been humbugged.

A few days later, Barnum and Tom were invited to the palace a second time. On this visit Tom got to meet Bertie and also Bertie's sister, Vickie, the Princess Royal, who was three and a half.

When the queen introduced Tom to Bertie, she said, "General, this is the Prince of Wales."

"How are you, Prince?" said Tom, shaking the child's hand. Then he edged closer to the two-year-old to compare their height. "The prince is taller than I," said Tom, "but I feel as big as anybody." Tom then strutted proudly back and forth across the room. Everyone laughed.

The queen then introduced Tom to Vickie. Tom took the princess by the hand and invited her to sit on an elegant miniature couch that Barnum had brought to the palace for Tom's use. Then he took a seat next to her. After the two chatted briefly, Tom got up and happily performed some of his songs and dances for the princess.

Ice cream and cake were served to the group. Tom showed he was a hearty eater.

"Darling, what do you like to do best?" the queen asked Tom.

After thinking for a moment, Tom saw the opportunity for a pun. "I like to *draw*, and do very well," he said, with a mischievous grin.

In a Scottish kilt, Tom performs for Queen Victoria, her husband,
Prince Albert, and their children. ✦ *From* The Life of P. T. Barnum *(1855)*

The queen didn't get it. She took the word *draw*, as most people would, to mean to create a picture with a pencil or pen, to sketch. But Tom was using the word in a different sense. He meant he was skilled in *drawing* big crowds to his shows.

It didn't bother Tom that the queen failed to recognize his pun. He shrugged and moved on to another subject.

Before Barnum and Tom left the palace that afternoon, the queen sat Tom on her lap and pinned a gold brooch on his chest. It sparkled with rubies and other precious stones. Then she kissed him. This was surprising conduct for the queen of England, and Tom knew it. For perhaps the first time in his life, he was speechless.

"What d'you say?" Barnum asked.

"Thank you, ma'am," Tom said, when he had recovered himself. "I'll keep the pin as long as I live."

CHAPTER SIX

A Royal Treat

 FEW WEEKS LATER, when Queen Victoria invited Tom to Buckingham Palace a third time, Leopold, the king of Belgium, was there. Leopold was the queen's uncle.

The queen wanted Tom to sing a song for the king. She asked him what he wished to sing.

"'Yankee Doodle,'" Tom replied.

Barnum immediately recognized that this was likely a dreadful choice. Although the song was originally sung by the British as a way of mocking the unkempt American militia, once the American troops began to dominate the British during the American Revolution, they claimed the song as their own and in turn sang it to taunt their English enemies. Barnum feared that the queen would be offended by this selection.

But the queen didn't seem to mind at all. "That is a very pretty song, General," she said. "Sing it, if you please."

Tom gave an enthusiastic performance. When he had finished, the queen kissed Tom and gave him a gift that had been specially made for him—a gold pencil box with his initials engraved upon the lid.

"I know this will make you happy, General," she said, "because you told me how much you like to draw." Tom graciously thanked the queen, but he knew she still didn't understand his pun.

By this time, all of England was in love with Tom. After his three audiences with the queen, London newspapers called him "the Pet of the Palace." Pictures of Tom began showing up in shop windows. His likeness was reproduced on souvenir plates and mugs. London's pictorial papers competed for portraits of him. Tom Thumb dolls went on sale, and songs were written in his honor. Young boys and girls could dance to the music of "The General Tom Thumb Polka," written especially for children.

The interest that the queen had shown in Tom triggered a booming business at the Egyptian Hall, where he was appearing. To reinforce for the public Tom's popularity with royalty, Barnum placed an ornate display case in the theater's entrance corridor to exhibit some of the many exquisite gifts that Tom had received. These included the ruby brooch that the queen had bestowed on him, as well as gifts that had come from other members of the British royalty. Among these

The Egyptian Hall, where Tom performed with great success, was named for its Egyptian style of architecture and ornamentation. Besides its popularity as an entertainment center, the Egyptian Hall featured a collection of curiosities from North and South America, Africa, and the South Seas. ✦ *Arthur Lloyd Co.*

were a gold watch and chain, a turquoise snuffbox, and jeweled swords and pistols.

On the evenings that Tom performed at the Egyptian Hall, extra police had to be summoned to handle the huge crowds. As many as fifty or sixty horse-drawn carriages would be lined up in the street outside the theater while their owners watched the show. London had never seen anything like it. Week after week, the Egyptian Hall was packed, with ticket sales averaging an incredible five hundred dollars a night. Barnum's daily expenses for the rental of the Egyptian Hall, newspaper advertising and the printing of posters, and hotel accommodations for himself and the Strattons amounted to a mere fifty dollars. Barnum was awash in money.

Besides his theater appearances, Tom was invited to attend three or four private parties a week. For each of these, he and Barnum received a handsome fee.

Tom was delighted when children were present at these events. He felt much more at ease. A room crowded exclusively with adults could make him feel uncomfortable. He would sometimes become swamped in a sea of men's legs and women's dresses, which could push him against chairs and tables. But gatherings of children presented no such problem.

At this point, Tom was spending so much time amid the English nobility that Barnum decided the boy should travel in the same manner as lords and ladies. At the cost of about two thousand dollars, the showman purchased a fancy carriage for Tom, painted a deep blue and decorated with the motto GO AHEAD. Not much bigger than a baby carriage, the coach had windows of plate glass and an interior lined in silk. It was drawn by a pair of tiny Shetland ponies the size of large dogs. To serve as driver and footman, Barnum hired two small boys and dressed them in servants' uniforms.

"It will be the greatest hit in the universe, see if it ain't!" Barnum wrote to a friend. He was right, of course. Whenever Tom and his elegant coach with its two uniformed stablemen rumbled through the streets, curious Londoners stood along the curb and gaped.

Tom's tour of Europe was to continue for two more years. He was proving to be such an enormous success that Barnum felt obliged to change his employment

Tom and his splendid coach, drawn by tiny Shetland ponies, created great excitement whenever they appeared on the streets of London. ✦ Bridgeport Public Library Historical Collection

status. Instead of being a paid employee, Tom was made an equal partner in their enterprise. Half of all profits would now go to Tom and his parents. As a result, seven-year-old Tom was well on his way to becoming a millionaire and thereby one of the wealthiest Americans of the nineteenth century.

No matter how much he earned or how much he received as an allowance, Tom was a penny-pincher. He liked to save, watch the funds accumulate, and

avoid spending. He would buy delicious pastries for himself or an occasional gift for his mother but little else.

Tom's passion for thrift was on display one Sunday afternoon when the Strattons were still in England and Barnum took Tom to London's Regent Park. There, for a shilling (about twenty-five cents), one could ride on the back of a huge elephant. The ride was one of Tom's favorite treats, and he would squeal with delight as he mounted the huge creature. Barnum liked the ride too.

One Sunday, Barnum decided to have some fun at Tom's expense. "I declare, I've forgotten my pocketbook," the showman said. "What are we going to do?" And he began turning his pockets inside out.

A look of distress crossed Tom's face. "Oh, Mr. Barnum," he said. "Surely you could find two shillings."

"Nope," said Barnum, "not a cent on me. You'll have to do the treating today."

Tom scowled. "Wouldn't the keeper let us ride the elephant for nothing, Mr. Barnum, if you told him how you'd forgotten your pocketbook?"

"Oh, I'd be afraid to ask him," Barnum said. "I guess then, General, if you won't stand treat, we'll be going home." The showman turned as if to leave.

Slowly, Tom took out his little pocketbook and plucked two shillings out of it, which he handed to Barnum. They had their elephant ride, but for Tom the pleasure was greatly reduced.

For all their future outings together, Tom never failed to ask, "You're sure you have your pocketbook with you, Mr. Barnum?"

After Tom ended his appearances at the Egyptian Hall, Barnum arranged for him to perform in cities and towns outside London. They also included Scotland and Ireland in their travels.

Next, it was on to France. Early in 1845, Barnum and Tom called upon King Louis Philippe at the Tuileries Palace. Tom sang a song in French, proclaiming his love of France.

The king was unusually friendly toward Tom and more than once invited him to visit the royal family in their private quarters. During one of his visits, the king presented Tom with an ornamental stickpin used to hold a gentleman's necktie or cravat in place. The pin was encrusted with large diamonds and emeralds. But the king had not taken the trouble to have the gift crafted for someone of the General's size. That didn't bother Tom. He removed the pin he was wearing and fixed the king's gift in its place. It looked huge on Tom's tiny chest.

During their stay in France, Barnum received the king's permission to include Tom and his miniature coach in a procession of royal carriages through

Tom was seven years old and performing in Europe when this lithograph, depicting him in his famous Napoleon costume, was produced. "This remarkable prodigy is 12 years old and only 25 inches tall," read the original caption. ✦ *Collection of the John and Mable Ringling Museum of Art, Tibbals Digital Collection*

Paris. When the General and his coach rolled by, the French went wild. Thousands upon thousands of people filled the air with their cheers.

Barnum rented a Paris concert hall where Tom could perform for the public. Twice a day the auditorium was filled to capacity. The profits were even greater

When Tom and Barnum traveled to France, Barnum had Tom's coach and ponies shipped to Paris. There, in his small vehicle, he was invited to join the procession of royal carriages.
 Bridgeport Public Library Historical Collection

than they had been in London. Barnum had to hire a cab to get all the coins and bills back to his hotel each night.

Then Barnum made a bold move on Tom's behalf. He arranged for him to appear in a full-length drama on the theatrical stage in an effort to broaden his public appeal even further. Tom made his debut as a stage actor at the Vaudeville Theatre in Paris in May 1845, in a play titled *Le Petit Poucet* (The Little Thumb).

Based on an ancient fairy tale made popular by Charles Perrault, the play tells the story of tiny Poucet, who like the character from Henry Fielding's *Tom Thumb*, was no bigger at birth than a man's thumb. He was one of seven children in a poor woodcutter's family. No longer able to provide for their children, the parents decide to abandon them. But the wise Poucet thwarts their plan and the children are reunited

In this illustration by Gustave Doré from *Le Petit Poucet*, tiny Poucet saves his siblings from an evil giant. ✦ *Wikimedia Commons*

with their parents, who are overjoyed at having them back. Poucet later outwits a wicked giant to save his own life and the lives of his siblings.

The play gave Tom the chance to display his talents not only as a singer, dancer, and comic, but as an actor. He was a sensation. The critics compared him favorably to leading professional actors of the day. Before he left France, he was elected to membership in the French Dramatic Society.

After Paris, the ever-active Barnum arranged a tour of France outside the French capital for Tom. The two then visited Belgium and Spain. Tom was a guest of fifteen-year-old Queen Isabella at Pamplona, in northern Spain.

In his performance before the queen, Tom appeared in a red and white clown suit. On his head he wore a tall pointed hat decorated with silver bells. It was the type of costume that might be worn by a court jester.

During his performance, he tipped his head from side to side to make the bells jingle. He began by singing a new version of "Yankee Doodle":

> *I'm General Thumb, just come to town,*
> *Yankee Doodle dandy.*
> *I've paid a visit to the Crown,*
> *Dressed like any grandee;*
> *The queen has made me presents rare,*
> *Court ladies did salute me.*
> *First rate I am, they all declare,*

And all my costumes suit me.
Yankee Doodle loves you all,
Yankee Doodle dandy.
Both young and old, and short and tall,
Declare that I'm a dandy.

Then Tom strutted about, did impersonations, danced, and sang some more songs. He had the queen laughing until tears streamed down her cheeks.

Wanting to see Tom again, she invited him to the bullfights with her. The queen's mother frowned. How could her daughter allow herself to be seen in public with a common little actor? But the queen had made up her mind. And she didn't merely attend the bullfights with Tom. Once she and her party were seated in the royal box and the parade of bullfighters had begun, she picked him up and placed him on her lap.

"Now I have the best seat of all," Tom said.

By the spring of 1846, Tom and Barnum were back in England. Tom appeared again at the Egyptian Hall. Barnum also arranged for Tom to continue his acting career, this time for English audiences, by appearing in a play titled *Hop o' My Thumb*, an adaptation of *Le Petit Poucet*.

Hop o' My Thumb was filled with zany humor. Tom was passed between the legs of a line of ballet dancers, dragged about in a wooden shoe, and

served up in a pie. He also got to sing "Yankee Doodle" and drive off in his famous miniature coach with its four Shetland ponies.

The English critics loved the show. The *London Times* reported, "The little General gave the greatest delight to audiences." The *Illustrated London News* hailed Tom for his "stage tact and comic humor." After six weeks in London, Tom toured in the play, taking it to several towns outside the city.

On Tom's return to London, Barnum began making plans to go back to America. But before they left, he booked Tom for a series of farewell appearances in the Egyptian Hall.

In a letter he later wrote to a minister in Albany, New York, Tom described his European tour: "I have traveled fifty thousand miles," he wrote, "been before more crowned heads than any other Yankee living except my friend Mr. Barnum, and have kissed nearly two million ladies, including the Queens of England, France, Belgium, and Spain."

On February 4, 1847, Tom, his parents, and Barnum boarded the packet *Cambria* for their return to New York.

CHAPTER SEVEN

Growing Up

EVERAL WEEKS before leaving Europe, Tom had celebrated his ninth birthday. By Barnum's standards, however, he was now fifteen years old, and the showman publicized him as such. Though Tom had not added so much as an inch in height during the three years he spent in Europe, he was a very grown up age nine. The years abroad had matured him. In Barnum's words, Tom was "cuter than ever" and "an educated, accomplished little man." Barnum might have added that he was also an experienced and canny stage performer.

His friends and acquaintances back in the United States remembered him as a little four-year-old. Though mischievous, he was often shy. He was much dif-

ferent now. His shyness had faded. He was sharper and wittier. He spoke French and Spanish and could play the violin.

Other nine-year-olds went to school and played with their school friends. But Tom had never gone to school; he had always had tutors. And his friends were almost all adults, not other children.

The great success he had achieved in Europe made Tom and his parents wealthy. It also benefited Tom himself in other ways. Through his talents as an actor, singer, dancer, and comic, he not only had managed to escape the harsher conditions that some dwarfs endured, but had also become a star.

Tom was content. By now, he was able to deal with most of the physical and emotional aspects of being very short. He was used to people patting the top of his head. There was always someone who was willing to get something for him from a top shelf.

Early in his life, Tom had been stared at, pointed at, and even laughed at without fail. But it was different now. He remembered an incident that took place on the day he arrived back in New York after his European tour, which had been thoroughly covered by the New York press. When Tom's carriage left the pier where the *Cambria* had docked, it was instantly recognized. Small boys ran alongside the vehicle, calling out to him. People stood on sidewalks and waved. "Welcome home, Tom!" he heard people shout.

He had been singled out and shouted at once again, but this time, it was not merely because he was tiny. Now he was a famous person, a celebrity. People admired and respected him.

Tom also noticed that his sisters' attitude toward him had changed. Before he left home for Europe, at times the girls had seemed uncomfortable with Tom, especially when they were in the company of their friends. Now it was obvious that Jennie, thirteen, and Libbie, eleven, felt quite sisterly toward him and were truly astonished at all that he had accomplished. Their warm feelings toward Tom may have arisen partly because some of his earnings would send them to fashionable private schools.

Hardly had Tom set foot in New York before Barnum booked him for four weeks of performances at his museum. Enormous crowds turned out to see him. To Barnum's great joy, the General shattered all museum box-office records for the four-week period.

After his month of performing was over, Tom returned to Bridgeport for a vacation. So many Bridgeporters wanted to see him that, before he could rest, he gave two performances for the general public at Bridgeport's Franklin Hall. Tom donated the three hundred dollars in ticket sales to the Ladies' Charitable Society.

With some of the profits from the European tour, Tom and his parents began building an impressive three-story mansion for the family on the northern edge of Bridgeport. The house included a separate apartment for Tom, with the rooms

and furniture scaled to his size. His father made miniature chests of drawers and kitchen cabinets for him. The lighting fixtures, doorknobs, and closet shelves were placed low to the floor. Tom slept in a little rosewood bed imported from France, a gift from Barnum. He also had a tiny billiard table. Billiards was one of Tom's favorite pastimes and he spent hours at the game.

After a month or so in Bridgeport, Tom, his parents, and Barnum set out on a yearlong American tour. They visited most of the large cities and a number of small towns east of the Mississippi River. They managed to take in Canada and Cuba too. In Washington, D.C., they met President James K. Polk and his wife.

When the tour came to an end, Barnum told Tom and his parents that he would no longer be accompanying them. "For thirteen years, I've been a traveling showman," Barnum said. "It's time I become acquainted with my family again." Barnum was to carry on his partnership with the Strattons, however, and continue to share in the profits that Tom generated.

Barnum did still keep active on Tom's behalf. It was under the showman's management that Tom played the title role in a number of full-scale stage productions, just as he had done with great success in England and France. Barnum arranged for Tom to make his American stage debut in *Hop o' My Thumb*. The play opened at the Broadway Theater in New York City in December 1848.

As he had in Europe, Tom won the acclaim of the critics. According to the *New York Herald*, "General Tom Thumb performed admirably and gave infinite

On Tom's return from Europe, some of the money that he had earned was used to build this stylish Bridgeport home for him and his father, mother, and sisters. The identity of the children posed in front of the house has been lost to history. ✦ *Bridgeport Public Library Historical Collection*

satisfaction to the audience. . . . It is really wonderful to see him." In the years after, Tom continued to star in *Hop* often, not only in Broadway theaters but also at Barnum's American Museum.

During the early 1850s, when Barnum was involved with other activities, Tom toured on his own, traveling from city to city with an entourage that included a valet to attend to his personal needs, a tutor, and an uncle who served as a ticket taker.

In September 1852, while Tom was on tour, a second son was born to the Strattons. Like Tom's sisters, the boy, named William, was of normal size. The following year, Tom's sister Libbie, now eighteen, married William Bassett, a New York leather merchant. After the joy of William's birth and Libbie's wedding, tragedy struck the Strattons: Tom's father died of a heart attack in December 1855.

After his father's passing, Tom's tours were managed by Libbie's husband. Sometimes Tom's mother went along, but she often preferred to remain at home and care for young William. Tom's valet and tutor continued to travel with him.

Tom enjoyed the life he was leading—the privileged treatment and the adulation. But more and more he believed his success was due not to his smallness but to his gifts as a mimic, comedian, and actor. Surely the warm

By the time he had reached his teens, Tom had his own valet and agents to handle his stage appearances and travel arrangements. By his late teens, he also had added three inches to his height.
◆ *Houghton Library, Harvard Theatre Collection*

praise he had received as a performer in *Hop o' My Thumb* and other stage productions helped shape the way he had come to regard himself.

What was perhaps Tom's most ambitious undertaking as a stage actor took place at Barnum's museum in the fall of 1856, when he appeared in a play titled *Dred; A Tale of the Great Dismal Swamp*. The play was based on a novel of the same name by Harriet Beecher Stowe, the famous author of *Uncle Tom's Cabin*.

Barnum had Stowe's novel adapted for the stage by H. J. Conway, a veteran playwright. In reshaping the book, Conway omitted many of the characters, changed the personalities of others, wrote in new characters, left out situations and incidents, and invented new ones.

In the Conway version of *Dred*, Tom played Tom Tit, a bright, handsome, and "upper crust" slave child. Though he was a minor character in the book, Tom Tit was seldom offstage in the play. He danced, sang gospel songs, and provided much of the play's comedy.

To play Tom Tit, the General performed in blackface, a popular tradition in American theater in the nineteenth century. To play black characters, white actors would apply burnt cork or black shoe polish to darken their skin and exaggerate the shape of their lips. Blackface actors often wore wigs, gloves, and ragged clothes to complete their look.

On stage, blackface characters were almost always the same: lazy, slow witted, clownish; sometimes they lied and stole. Through the years, these roles were

This photograph of Tom in Highland dress, entitled "Wee Laddie," shows his playful stage presence. ✦ *London Stereoscopic Company/Getty Images*

extremely influential in promoting racist images and attitudes toward African Americans. Though the practice of blackface is unacceptable today, most people of the 1850s saw it as harmless entertainment, and those who performed in blackface did not necessarily see themselves as promoting negative stereotypes. It's difficult to know what eighteen-year-old Charley Stratton felt about race, but

his thoughts on slavery may have been influenced by Barnum. Although in the 1830s Barnum had owned three slaves—a woman, a child, and a male personal valet, as well as, on paper, anyway, Joice Heth—by the 1850s he was an outspoken abolitionist, bent on seeking a legal end to slavery.

In reviewing *Dred*, newspaper critics had only praise for Tom. One critic noted that he was "the most unique feature of the whole thing" and concluded that the General had made a decided hit. Another hailed Tom as "an American institution, one of the greatest idols of American audiences," and a "mighty little star."

Despite the lavish praise, Tom's career as a performer in full-length plays never went beyond *Dred; A Tale of the Great Dismal Swamp* and *Hop o' My Thumb*. He knew his limitations. He had no wish to attempt any part not especially written for a person of short stature.

After *Dred*, Tom went back to touring, giving performances at Barnum's Lecture Room and elsewhere. He began each program by giving his account of his travels in Europe and his encounters with European royalty. He went on to perform his imitations of Napoleon, Frederick the Great, and others that had been so popular in the past. He sang and danced.

In 1855, Tom began to hear rumors that Barnum was having serious financial problems.

By mid-January 1856, the news was out: Barnum had lost almost everything

THE ORIGINAL AND CELEBRATED

GENERAL TOM THUMB,

THE WORLD-RENOWNED

American Man in Miniature.

This is the same remarkable LITTLE MAN, who was first introduced to the public by P. T. BARNUM, Esq., at his American Museum, New York, on the 8th day of December, 1842, and who, after receiving the adulations of thousands of ladies and gentlemen in the United States, visited Europe, appeared on FOUR different occasions before Her Majesty Queen Victoria, and the Royal Family, as well as nearly all the Crowned Heads of Europe, and Twenty Millions of Persons.

He last summer returned from a second tour through Great Britain, Germany, Holland, and France, and having long since acquired a fortune, he has been trying for the second time to content himself by retiring to private life. He finds, however, that SEVENTEEN YEARS OF PUBLIC LIFE have served to render the excitement attendant thereon, necessary to his happiness, and for this reason he has determined to make one more Tour through the United States, including California, after which he contemplates visiting Australia, and returning again to England.

The little General's outfit on this occasion is of the most splendid and superb description. His entire entertainment is elegant, unique, amusing, and enchanting. He spares no pains nor expense to render it worthy of the patronage and attention of all classes.

Since his last appearance in this country, the little General's intellect has vastly expanded. He has also added to his attractions a great variety of New Songs, Dances, Imitations, and Performances in numerous Costumes.

RARE COMBINATION OF NOVELTIES!

GENERAL TOM THUMB,

SENOR OLIVEIRA,

The Great Violinist and Second Paganini,

MR. WILLIAM TOMLIN,

Baritone, from the Nobility's Concerts, London,

AND THE CELEBRATED PIANIST,

C. C. TITCOMB,

Late of the Academy of Music, who will appear at each Entertainment.

Lyceum Hall, Lynn,

FRIDAY & SATURDAY, JULY 27 & 28.

For TWO DAYS Only.

Two Entertainments every day, from 3 to 4½ o'clock, and 8 to 9½ o'clock. Ladies and families will find the Morning Entertainment the more appropriate time for their visit, as they will avoid the crowd and confusion of the Evening.

One of Chickering's Celebrated Pianos will be used at each Entertainment.

This CHARMING MAN IN MINIATURE, is undoubtedly by far the SMALLEST MAN ALIVE, of his age. He is intelligent, sprightly, educated, perfectly symmetrical in all his proportions, and graceful beyond belief.

HE IS 22 YEARS OLD, AND WEIGHS 33 POUNDS.

He appears in a great variety of interesting Performances, Imitations, Costumes, Songs, Dances, &c., &c., including,

Napoleon Bonaparte, Frederick the Great, The Oxonian, Sailor, Grecian Statues, Highland Chieftain, Bobbing around, Villikins and his Dinah, The Court Dress worn before Her Majesty, The Polka, Highland Fling, &c., &c.

His entertainments are interspersed with the delightful musical performances of Senor Oliveira, the great Violinist, and Mr. Wm. Tomlin, the Vocalist.

THE MAGNIFICENT JEWELS, &c., &c.,

Presented to him by Queen Victoria, and the Crowned Heads of Europe, are exhibited at each entertainment.

The General's Beautiful Equipage,

Consisting of Miniature Chariot drawn by the

SMALLEST PONIES IN THE WORLD.

And attended by ELFIN COACHMAN and FOOTMAN in livery, will promenade the Public Streets on the day of Exhibition. When the weather is pleasant, the GENERAL RIDES in his LITTLE CARRIAGE to and from the Hall of Exhibition.

The Little General is no longer under an engagement to any individual, but gives his Exhibitions solely on his own account. At the close of each Exhibition, the General will supply his visitors cost price) with Photographs and Medals, representing him in his various Characters; also, with his Book, containing an account of his History, Family and Travels as well as all of his SONGS. He gives his portrait (BARNUM RECEIPT to each Lady purchaser as may desire it. His Performances are accompanied with Music.

ADMISSION:

Day Entertainment	·	·	24 cts.	Evening Entertainment	·	·	25 cts.
Children under 10 years,	·	·	18 "	Children under 10 years,	·	·	16 "
				Reserved Seats,	·	·	25 "

Box Office open from 9 A M to 4 P.M.

---

in a real estate venture that failed. As early as 1851, Barnum had begun to invest heavily in the development of a brand-new city just across the Pequonnock River from Bridgeport. Called East Bridgeport, it was to have its own schools and churches, homes and factories. He poured money into the project. In one effort to attract new business to the site, he made a substantial investment in what turned out to be a worthless clock company. When the company went bankrupt, so did Barnum's real estate company. All of his profits

Touring on his own in Lynn, Massachusetts, Tom headed a program that included several musical acts and also presented his "miniature chariot," touted as "being drawn by the smallest ponies in the world." ✦ *Bridgeport Public Library Historical Collection*

from the museum and his long relationship with Tom were gone. Barnum was bankrupt.

Fortunately, many of the performers, actors, and theater owners who had known Barnum came forward to offer help. Tom was one of them. He was in Philadelphia on tour when news of Barnum's distress reached him. He sat down and wrote a letter to his friend. It was not without puns:

> *My Dear Mr. Barnum: I understand your friends, and that means "all creation," intend to get up some benefits for your family. Now, my dear sir, just be good enough to remember that I belong to that mighty crowd, and I must have a finger (or at least a "thumb") in that pie.*
>
> *. . . I have just started out on my western tour, and I have my carriages, ponies and assistants all here, but I am ready to go to New York, and remain at Mr. Barnum's service as long as I, in my small way, can be useful.*

At first, Barnum said no to Tom's offer of help. But when Tom suggested that Barnum tour Europe again with him and share the profits, Barnum changed his answer to yes.

Barnum sailed for London late in 1856. Tom arrived not long after New Year's Day in 1857. On January 4, he turned nineteen. After his fifteenth birthday, Tom had begun to grow slowly. By the time he was eighteen, he had added three inches to his height, making him twenty-eight inches tall. But he was still very much the "man in miniature," and, as one British paper described him, "the same rollicking, jolly little blade."

After performances in London and a tour of England, Tom returned to France. He then made his first visits to Germany and Holland before going back to London.

Since Tom was now mature enough to handle matters on his own, Barnum did not always accompany him. The showman made several return trips to America while Tom toured. He left trusted associates to assist him.

By the end of 1859, Tom and Barnum were back in America. With what he earned from the tour and other sources, Barnum was able to pay off most of his debts, though it took him four years to do so. In March 1860, ready to make his museum bigger and better than ever, he took out advertisements in New York newspapers that proclaimed, "Barnum is on his feet again."

Tom's latest European tour had boosted his wealth. He began to overcome his unwillingness to spend money. He invested in real estate in and around Bridgeport. He hired servants and acquired a number of fine horses, quartering them in a stable he built. Yachting was now his favorite sport. He loved sailing his splendid boat on Long Island Sound. At one stage he thought he might turn the activity into a profitable business. He even went so far as to propose trading a fast sloop he owned for a small steamer that he planned to use to tow vessels in and

By 1860, the approximate date of this photograph taken by Mathew Brady, Barnum, after several troublesome years, had emerged from bankruptcy— with Tom's help—and was his confident self once more.

✦ *National Portrait Gallery, Smithsonian Institution*

out of Bridgeport Harbor. Tom began to spend as much time with his expensive toys as he did on tour.

Although he had been dealt a difficult hand, Tom had led a good life so far. With his fine clothes, splendid home, bulging bank account, and many playthings, he had achieved all he had ever hoped to achieve, and more. But something was missing.

Lavinia

N HIS STAGE performances at Barnum's American Museum and other playhouses, Tom often sang this song, which he had made popular:

> *I should like to marry if I could only find*
> *Any pretty lady, suited to my mind;*
> *I should like her handsome, I should like her good,*
> *With a little money—yes, indeed I should.*
> *Oh! then I would marry, if I could but find*
> *Any pretty lady suited to my mind.*

At the end, the audience roared with laughter. Tom laughed too.

But he was really not amused by the song. It spoke the truth. His fame and wealth were not enough. Often he was lonely. Surely, if he could find "a pretty lady," "handsome" and "good," he would happily marry her.

While Tom had met and kissed many thousands of women, he never had had a girlfriend, either of short stature or otherwise. Now, at age twenty-four, he had begun to believe that making a good match or finding a lifetime partner was impossible.

Then Tom's world changed: he met Lavinia.

Beginning in the fall of 1862 and stretching into the winter of 1863, Tom was on vacation at his home in Bridgeport, resting from the rigors of touring. From time to time, he would travel into New York City for a day. There he would visit his sister Libbie, who lived in the Chelsea section of the city. He also liked to drop in at the museum to chat with his friend Barnum.

On one such visit early in 1863, twenty-one-year-old Lavinia was performing on the museum's Lecture Room stage. Lavinia was born Mercy Lavinia Warren Bump in the small Massachusetts town of Middleboro on October 31, 1841. Only thirty-two inches tall, she was perfectly formed, a woman in miniature. She was bright and attractive, talented, and fond of poetry, music, and the other fine arts.

Lavinia was the fifth child in a family of eight children. All were of normal size except Lavinia and the youngest child. Minnie, born in 1849, was eight years younger than Lavinia and even smaller.

When Lavinia was sixteen, the country school that she was attending expanded in size. The school board offered to make her a primary grade teacher, and she accepted. Even the youngest child in her class was taller than Lavinia.

She didn't let that bother her. "I was," she said, "very zealous in my duty."

Her students were deeply fond of her. In the harsh Massachusetts winter, they hauled her through the snow by sled and carried her into the school to keep her feet dry. In the classroom, her pupils were, as she put it, "anxious to be obedient" and to please her. Lavinia felt that she had found a lifelong career.

A visit from a cousin early in 1858 made her change her mind. The cousin was the manager of a showboat, a traveling theater that plied the Mississippi, Ohio, and various western rivers, stopping at cities along the route. The showboat offered two main attractions. One was a theater where performers staged minstrel shows—entertainment that consisted of comedy routines and songs and dances performed by people in blackface. The other attraction was a museum, or what the cousin called a "floating palace of curiosities." It was, quite simply, a freak show.

The cousin invited Lavinia to join the showboat cast, to sing, dance, and meet the paying customers. It sounded exciting to the sixteen-year-old Lavinia. She liked the idea of being way "out West" and sailing "the beautiful Ohio" and "the mighty Mississippi," and she was eager to accept her cousin's offer.

When Lavinia went to her parents to ask their permission to join the show-

At twenty-one, Lavinia Warren Bump was thirty-two inches in height and weighed twenty-nine pounds. After Barnum hired Lavinia, he convinced her to drop the surname Bump.
♦ *Library of Congress*

boat troupe, they were shocked she would even consider the idea. A stormy family meeting followed. Lavinia pleaded tearfully. One of her brothers threatened to leave home and never return if Lavinia went through with her plan. Only when her cousin promised to keep Lavinia under his personal supervision and cousinly care did her parents reluctantly relent. Lavinia left home the next morning, not wanting to give them a chance to reconsider.

On board the showboat, Lavinia shared a stateroom with another performer, a giantess who was nearly seven feet tall, with whom she became close friends. On stage, Lavinia sang songs such as "The Cottage by the Sea" and "Annie of the Vale." But she spent most of her time in conversation with audience members.

Lavinia's career as a showboat entertainer was overshadowed by the excitement and fears stirred by the approaching conflict between North and South, especially after the election of Abraham Lincoln in 1860. Tensions were mounting when the showboat was on the Mississippi River in the Deep South. Southerners began seizing every small boat and river steamer for military use. As Northerners, the crew and acting troupe worried that they would be stranded in enemy territory.

As their fears grew, Lavinia's cousin took charge. He led Lavinia and other members of the showboat cast to Vicksburg, Mississippi, where they managed to board a steamer bound for the safety of Louisville, Kentucky. In

⦿ ⦿ ⦿ AN IMPORTANT FRIEND ⦿ ⦿ ⦿

On Lavinia's first trip up the Mississippi River, the showboat stopped at Galena, Illinois, for three days. One day during its stay a clerk in a local leather store visited the showboat and asked to meet Lavinia. When they were introduced, he gave his name as Sam Grant. He explained he had been reading about her in the

newspapers. The two chatted like old friends. Before Grant left, he purchased a photograph of Lavinia and asked her to autograph it. The next day, Grant brought his family to meet Lavinia. Rather than watch the show being performed that day, they talked with Lavinia. Warm wishes were exchanged when the Grants left.

When the Civil War broke out, Sam Grant, as General Ulysses S. Grant, emerged as the great military leader of the Union. Still later, he became the eighteenth U.S. president.

Library of Congress

⦿ ⦿ ⦿ ⦿ ⦿

Louisville, Lavinia said goodbye to her cousin and took the first available train for Middleboro and home.

Lavinia spent several weeks recovering from her ordeal, then began making occasional appearances at freak shows offered at state and county fairs in the region. Amid games of skill and chance, shooting galleries, variety acts, wax museums, and mechanical rides, Lavinia was exhibited with other "human oddities"— the usual assortment of fat people, thin people, people born with missing limbs, people with excess hair, people with tattoos, and Native Americans—exactly the sort of appearances Barnum strove to avoid for Tom. If this experience caused her to feel any loss of dignity, Lavinia never voiced it.

Lavinia and her parents first heard from Barnum in the summer of 1862 when he sent an agent to the Bump family home in Middleboro to meet and talk with her. After the agent reported back to Barnum, he returned to Middleboro to negotiate with the Bumps for Lavinia to make a series of appearances at the American Museum, to be followed by a tour of Europe.

But the Bumps were not thrilled by the offer. They were suspicious of Barnum. They undoubtedly had heard of the Joice Heth hoax and the deception surrounding the Fejee Mermaid. They were afraid, said Lavinia, that she would "be looked upon as another of Barnum's 'humbugs.'" When Barnum learned of the Bumps' misgivings, he immediately invited Lavinia and her parents to come to Bridgeport and meet with him at his mansion.

Barnum was persuasive, and in the end Lavinia signed a long-term contract with him. Since Barnum didn't consider the name Bump suitable for show business, he got her to agree to be known as Lavinia Warren.

Barnum's daughter Libbie helped her father pick out the clothes and costumes that Lavinia would need for her stage appearances. Libbie also advised him as to what jewelry would be suitable for the dainty woman. Once her wardrobe was complete, Barnum arranged a number of receptions for Lavinia at the St. Nicholas, New York City's most luxurious hotel, where she met members of the press. Following one such reception, the *New York Tribune* noted Lavinia's "full, round dimpled face" and stated that "her fine black eyes fairly sparkle when she becomes interested in conversation. . . . Her voice is soft and sweet, and she sings excellently well."

On January 2, 1863, Lavinia made her debut on the Lecture Room stage in the first of a series of "levees" in which she sang, danced, and exchanged light and playful remarks with members of the audience.

One day shortly after her first appearance at the museum, Tom saw Lavinia perform. When she had finished, he immediately went backstage to introduce himself. Afterward, almost in a daze, he hurried to Barnum's office. He was highly excited, Barnum recalled. Tom inquired about Lavinia's family and Barnum told him what he knew. Then Tom said, "Mr. Barnum, that is the most charming little lady I ever saw, and I believe she was created on purpose to be my

wife! Now," he continued, "you have always been a friend of mine, and I want you to say a good word for me to her. I have got plenty of money and I want to marry and settle down in life, and I really feel as if I must marry that young lady."

Barnum frowned. He told Tom that he was acting with too much haste. While the showman was well aware of the publicity that could be generated by such a match, he advised Tom "to take time to think of it."

But Tom insisted that even years of thought would make no difference. His mind was made up.

In the weeks that followed, Tom visited the museum often to meet with Lavinia. The couple also spent Sunday afternoons and evenings together. Tom seemed to be making progress in his courtship. But there was a problem. Barnum had earlier hired a dwarf, of twenty-nine inches in height, named George Washington Morrison Nutt, whom he exhibited at the museum. Barnum gave him the title Commodore, a naval rank just above captain, and had him dress in a naval uniform. After signing him to a three-year contract at ten thousand dollars a year, Barnum publicized him as the "$30,000 Nutt."

Commodore Nutt also developed a crush on Lavinia. His rivalry with Tom for Lavinia's affections even led to a scuffle in a museum dressing room. The Commodore, wiry and quick, threw Tom down on his back. After that, Tom, a man of peace, kept a good distance from the hotheaded Commodore.

Then Barnum invited Lavinia, Tom, and the Commodore to spend the weekend at his Bridgeport mansion. Tom arrived before the Commodore and quickly swung into action.

He and Lavinia were playing backgammon in the mansion's sitting room. Tom eventually brushed the game board aside and suggested they talk. Two young women, also houseguests of Barnum, overheard their conversation and passed their words on to the showman.

Tom drew his chair closer to Lavinia's. "So you're going to Europe soon," Tom said.

"Yes," Lavinia replied, "Mr. Barnum intends to take me in a couple of months."

"You will find it very pleasant," said Tom. "I have been there twice, in fact. I spent six years abroad, and I like the old countries very much."

"I hope I shall like the trip, and I expect I shall."

"I wish I was going over, for I know all about the countries, and I could explain them all to you."

"That would be very nice."

"Would you really like to have me go?" Tom asked, slipping his arm around Lavinia's waist.

"Of course I would."

"Don't you think it would be pleasanter if we went as man and wife?"

Lavinia was startled. She quickly moved Tom's arm away from her waist and told the General she didn't like it when he joked in such a way.

"I'm not joking at all," Tom said. "It's quite too serious a matter for that."

Lavinia thought for a few seconds, then said, "I think I love you well enough to consent, but I have always said that I would never marry without my mother's consent."

Now Tom was grinning. "Oh! I'll ask your mother. May I do that, pet?"

"Yes, Tom, you may ask my mother."

Kissing followed, the eavesdroppers reported.

Tom wasted no time in meeting with Lavinia's parents. "I have felt that kind heaven designed her for my partner in life," he told them. "I assure you that if she becomes my wife, I shall do all in my power to make her happy." Mrs. Bump gave her approval of the marriage, although she was quite distressed by the mustache that Tom had grown.

The wedding date was set for Tuesday, February 10, 1863. The ceremony was to be held at New York's Grace Church on Broadway at Twelfth Street.

Announcement of the event caused great excitement. Lavinia's appearances at the museum became "crowded to suffocation," Barnum noted. Ticket sales

When Barnum introduced the twenty-nine-inch-tall Commodore Nutt to the public in 1862, he had no idea that this performer would later rival Tom for Lavinia's affection. ✦ *The Rail Splitter Collection*

swelled to three thousand dollars a day. With that kind of income, Barnum was happy to pay all the wedding expenses. He promised to keep the ceremony elegant and refined, though earlier he had considered selling tickets to the event.

As the money poured in, Barnum went to the General with an offer. If he and Lavinia would agree to postpone the wedding for a month and continue their exhibitions at the museum, he would pay them fifteen thousand dollars.

Tom shook his head. "Not for fifty thousand dollars," he said. Lavinia agreed.

"The Fairy Wedding," as it was called, took place as scheduled. Commodore Nutt, who had painfully accepted Lavinia's decision to marry Tom, agreed to serve as Tom's best man. Barnum tried to ease the Commodore's suffering. He suggested that Lavinia's young sister, Minnie, even tinier than Lavinia herself, would be a better match. Barnum said, "She is a charming little creature, and two years younger than you, while Lavinia is several years your senior." But the Commodore felt that Minnie was not an adequate replacement for Lavinia, his one true love. Minnie did end up as a member of the wedding party, however, as Lavinia's maid of honor.

The event was not merely a wedding. It was one of the most notable happenings of 1863. The Civil War was raging, and the North had recently suffered a terrible defeat at Fredericksburg, Virginia. On New Year's Day, President

Lincoln had issued the Emancipation Proclamation, declaring the freedom of all slaves in states that had seceded from the Union. "The Fairy Wedding" provided a welcome distraction and rivaled the war for space in the *New York Times* and other newspapers across the nation.

On the morning of the wedding, surging crowds of people filled the streets near the church. The police put up barricades and formed human chains in an effort to control the mob.

At noon a miniature wedding carriage bearing the bride and groom pulled up to the church. Inside, more than two thousand guests waited. They included governors, members of Congress, and hundreds of New York's most elegant citizens.

The bride was dressed in a gown of splendid white satin with a lace veil. She wore a diamond necklace and diamond pins that Tom had given her as wedding gifts. Tom looked courtly in a full dress suit of rich black cloth, a vest of white silk, white gloves, and shiny boots.

After the couple made their way down the center aisle and approached the altar, they climbed six short steps to a carpeted platform. The raised surface enabled the guests to see them.

Barnum arranged for official wedding photographs of the couple to be taken several days before the actual event. He was then able to sell copies of the pictures to the public the instant the ceremony ended.

Mathew Brady, the famous Civil War photographer who had photographed

A Fairy Wedding

The bride, Lavinia Warren (left).
♦ *Author's collection*

The maid of honor, Minnie
Warren (right). ♦ *Author's collection*

The maid of honor and best man, Minnie Warren and
Commodore Nutt. ✦ *Author's collection*

The bride and groom, Mr. and Mrs. Tom Thumb.

✦ *New York Public Library*

Abraham Lincoln and countless other notables of the time, made the wedding portraits. He photographed the wedding party in his studio across Broadway from Grace Church. Placing Tom and the others in front of a backdrop meant to look like the interior of the church, Brady created the illusion that the photographs had been taken during the actual service.

In the photographs, it is obvious that Tom had added several inches to his height since his teenage years. From the rich food he enjoyed, he had also added inches to his waistline. The mustache that so distressed his mother-in-law made him look older than his twenty-five years. What *Harper's Weekly* referred to as his "prettiness, brightness, and grace" was gone. His portly look did not seem to detract from interest in his wedding, however.

Small copies of the wedding photographs as well as individual portraits of Tom and Lavinia, and Commodore Nutt and Minnie Warren, were mounted on cardboard and mass produced as wedding souvenirs. Each image was about the size of a credit card and bore facsimile signatures of the participants on the reverse side.

These small cards, known as *cartes de visite*, were enormously popular in the 1860s. Images of prominent men and women were collected and traded, and sometimes saved and displayed in family photograph albums along with pictures of one's own family, relatives, and friends.

No one knows exactly how many copies of the wedding photographs were

made, but the number printed was in the tens of thousands. In his autobiography, Barnum noted that Lavinia's portrait cards were selling as many as twelve hundred a day even before the wedding. Original prints of the Thumbs are still available today from online auction houses and dealers in antiquarian photographs.

After the ceremony, the wedding carriage took the couple to the Metropolitan Hotel, where the reception was held. The couple's wedding gifts were on display in the hotel's spacious parlor. Mrs. August Belmont, the undisputed leader of New York society, gave Tom and Lavinia a necklace of Tuscan gold. Tiffany and Company, the famous jeweler, presented them with a miniature silver horse and chariot decorated with rubies. From Mrs. Lincoln, the president's wife, came an exquisite set of fireplace screens. Barnum gave the Thumbs a curious gift—a mechanical bird with natural feathers that sang sweet songs when a spring was touched.

The members of the wedding party made their way through the mass of well-wishers; then they were placed on the hotel's grand piano. From that perch, they greeted their guests with a smile, a wave, or a nod of the head.

The next day, the Thumbs set off on their wedding trip. They traveled to Philadelphia, where a reception was held in their honor, and then on to Washington. While in the nation's capital, they received an invitation from Mrs. Lincoln to be guests at a White House reception. Members of the president's cabinet were also invited.

The wedding reception was held at the Metropolitan Hotel on Broadway, where Tom and Lavinia greeted the guests from atop a grand piano. ✦ *Bridgeport Public Library Historical Collection*

After greeting the newlyweds, the president led Tom and Lavinia to a sofa, then lifted Tom up onto it. Mrs. Lincoln did the same for Lavinia. The Lincolns' ten-year-old son, Tad, looked curiously at the couple for a few moments, then glanced briefly at his father, whose height was six feet, four inches. He said, "Mother, isn't it funny that Father is so tall and Mr. and Mrs. Stratton are so little?"

The president overheard his son's remark. "My boy," he said, "it is because Dame Nature sometimes delights in doing funny things. You need not seek for any other reason, for here you have the *long* and the *short* of it."

Following their wedding trip, Tom and Lavinia settled down in Middleboro to rest after what Lavinia called "a season of hurry and excitement." There Lavinia reflected on all that had happened in her life during a period of only

A tiny brass photo album, less than an inch tall, containing souvenir pictures from the wedding and beyond (note the baby in the last photograph), speaks to the enormous popularity of Tom Thumb and his companions. ✦
Charles Schwartz Photography

eight months. She had been hired by Barnum, had begun performing at Barnum's American Museum, had met and married Tom Thumb after a whirlwind courtship, and had been welcomed at the White House by President and Mrs. Lincoln before returning to Middleboro to be warmly greeted by the townspeople. "Truly," said Lavinia, "it was a story from dreamland."

CHAPTER NINE

Touring Together

EWSPAPERS in every corner of the globe covered "The Fairy Wedding" at great length. Tom and Lavinia now reigned as the most famous couple on the face of the earth.

This truth did not escape Barnum, and he moved quickly to take advantage of their worldwide popularity. Before 1863 ended, Barnum had sent the wedding party on an extended tour. It took them through New England and the Midwest and into Canada.

Barnum was deeply involved with his museum during this time. Shortly after the Thumbs' wedding, he had brought in some of the most powerful Native American chiefs to appear on the museum's stage. They included White Bull, a nephew of Sitting Bull, and War Bonnet and Lean Bear of the Cheyennes.

Barnum picked Sylvester Bleeker, one of his most trusted associates, to man-

age the 1863 tour. A former actor, author, and stage manager, Bleeker had a close relationship not only with Barnum but with Tom and Lavinia as well. He also had roles on stage. He introduced the performers to the audience each evening and played the part of the Doctor, trading quips with Tom in his comic routines.

Toward the end of the tour, Tom admitted to Lavinia that he was weary of traveling. And for good reason. Now in his midtwenties, he had been on public display for the past twenty years. He was meeting and shaking hands with the sons and daughters, and even the grandsons and granddaughters, of people who had come to see him years before. Life as a performer was losing its appeal.

It was different for Lavinia. She loved traveling from place to place and thrived on the excitement of the crowds that met the group at railroad stations. She relished the cheers and applause that greeted their performances. As for the Commodore and Minnie, touring was a new experience for them, and they got as much delight from it as Lavinia did. Tom yielded to the wishes of the others and continued, willingly, to travel and perform.

When the tour ended in June 1864, Tom and Lavinia returned to Bridgeport for some rest and relaxation. Tom delighted in playing billiards, sailing his boat, and hitching up a matched pair of his fine horses to one of the handsome

Tom, Lavinia, and Minnie enjoyed a warm friendship with Sylvester Bleeker, who managed their tours. His wife served as the troupe's wardrobe mistress. ✦ *Bridgeport Public Library Historical Collection*

carriages he owned so he could whisk through the streets of Bridgeport.

Their vacation did not last long. Sylvester Bleeker visited the Thumbs in Bridgeport one day to inquire whether the couple wanted to make a tour of Europe that Barnum planned to arrange. Tom shrugged. He had been to Europe several times. The idea of another trip to the Continent held little appeal. But Lavinia was thrilled by the prospect of European travel. She reminded Tom that the earlier tour to England and France that Barnum had been planning for her had been called off because of their wedding.

"We'll go, won't we, darling?" asked Lavinia.

Tom could only answer yes. He would do almost anything to make Lavinia happy.

The Thumbs, along with the Commodore and Minnie, sailed for England on October 29, 1864. One facet of the tour was particularly notable. When Tom and Lavinia arrived in London, the Prince and Princess of Wales invited the couple to Marlborough House, their newly enlarged mansion, which had become the social center of the city. In their first meeting with the prince and princess, the Thumbs engaged in a bit of bold humbuggery that would have made Barnum proud and may, in fact, have been done with the showman's prompting. They carried with them a small baby wrapped in a blanket, whom they introduced as their infant daughter. Tom and Lavinia never had children of their own; the

On October 29, 1864, Tom and Lavinia Thumb and Minnie Warren said goodbye to family and friends on the quarterdeck of the steamer *City of Washington* as the vessel prepared to depart from New York for England. ✦ *Bridgeport Public Library Historical Collection*

baby was a hoax. Lavinia later admitted that the infant was borrowed from a foundling home.

The plot to deceive the public had been hatched before the Thumbs left for Europe. A photograph provides the evidence. It shows Lavinia posing with a child

The Thumbs never had any children. But before they left for England, they attempted to create the impression that they were parents by introducing a borrowed baby as their own. Selling small card photographs of themselves with "their" baby became a profitable sideline for Tom and Lavinia. ✦ *The Rail Splitter Collection*

in her arms, and its caption reads, "Gen. Tom Thumb's Wife & Child." The photograph's copyright was in the name of Mathew Brady, indicating that it was taken in New York before Tom and Lavinia's departure.

Tom and Lavinia promoted the humbug with an illustrated hand-bill that depicted the two of them, and the Commodore and Minnie, standing around a chair in which an infant, hailed as the "Wonder of the Age," is seated.

The child caused a sensation, as the Thumbs hoped it would. But as the infant grew, it created a prob-lem, for it began to rival both its "father" and "mother" in height and weight. The Thumbs didn't know quite what to do. They consulted

Here Lavinia coolly poses
with the humbug infant. ✦ *Author's collection*

147

Barnum, who suggested that they exchange the original baby for a younger, smaller one.

They followed this practice throughout their European tour. They were careful about the baby's nationality too. Local orphanages or foundling homes provided the Thumbs with an English baby in England, a French baby in France, and a German baby in Germany.

Tom and Lavinia arranged to have studio photographs of themselves taken with each of their babies. They sold *cartes de visite* of these photographs by the thousands at the end of their performances.

Meanwhile, while the Thumbs were on tour in Europe, Barnum was struck a heavy blow. In July 1865, his American Museum and most of its contents, including many animals, were destroyed by fire. The showman was quick to recover, however. Within six weeks, he had opened his New American Museum, locating it farther north on Broadway. (In March 1868, that too was ravaged by fire. That was enough for Barnum. He gave up the museum business for good.)

When the Thumbs' European tour ended in June 1867, and the last baby had been taken back to its foundling home, the Thumbs returned to Bridgeport. Tom was happy there. He could indulge in his favorite pastimes, one of which was now embroidery. Lavinia had taught him to use needle and thread to create ornamental designs on cloth. She and Tom worked together to make decorative coverings for a set of their upholstered furniture.

In this poster hailing their popularity with the royal families of Europe, Tom and Lavinia appear especially doll-like. ♦ *Collection of the John and Mable Ringling Museum of Art, Tibbals Digital Collection*

On July 13, 1865, while Tom and Lavinia were on tour in Europe,
a horrendous fire destroyed Barnum's American Museum. ✦ *Barnum Museum*

Less than two months after
his original American
Museum was devastated by
fire, Barnum was operating
a new museum on
Broadway at Spring Street.
It, too, was later
destroyed by fire.
✦ *New York Public Library*

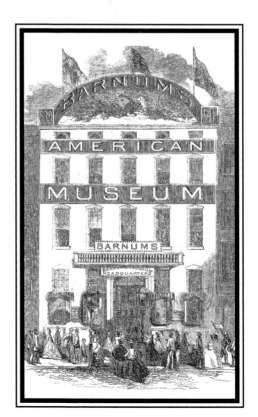

Tom also took great pleasure in being a seaman. But, for the time being, he had given up yachts and sailing in favor of a "vapor launch," a small motorized craft. Named the *Julie L.*, the boat was powered by an engine that burned naphtha, a gasoline-like fuel.

Tom enjoyed taking his friends on cruises out of Bridgeport into Long Island Sound. Sometimes he would head for the Thimble Islands, a group of a hundred or so small islands scattered in the sound at the mouth of Stony Creek, not far from the town of Branford. About two dozen of the islands were occupied. Tom liked to visit a cousin who is said to have lived in a quaint cottage on Cut-in-Two Island East, one of the Thimbles. Tom must have been a confident sailor, for underwater rock ledges make navigation around the Thimble Islands treacherous.

In Bridgeport, Tom spent hours at his toy-size billiard table and learned to play a miniature grand piano. The Thumbs also occupied themselves with the construction of a second mansion on Plymouth Street in Middleboro. It occupied a spacious plot of land diagonally across the street from the home of Lavinia's mother. The Thumbs planned to divide their leisure time between the new house in Middleboro and the older one in Bridgeport. It was in the Bridgeport home that Tom's mother and his brother, William, now a young teenager, continued to live.

Like the house in Bridgeport, Tom and Lavinia's house in Middleboro was scaled to their size. Windows were placed low to the floor. The topmost shelves

Tom and Lavinia pose with an unidentified woman in front of their elegant home in Middleboro, Massachusetts. Tom quartered his ponies and stored his carriages in the stable to the right of the house.

◆ *Bridgeport Public Library Historical Collection*

of cabinets and bookcases were within easy reach. Stairsteps were built closer together. Rooms were furnished with miniature chairs, tables, desks, and beds.

Though Tom had become tired of constant traveling, both he and Lavinia found it hard to settle down for extended periods. Lavinia, especially, itched to tour again. When Barnum came forward with another offer to resume touring, they agreed to do so. The Civil War had ended in April 1865, with the surrender of General Robert E. Lee. Though much of the South had been devastated, with farms and factories destroyed and many city and towns leveled, Barnum was convinced it was possible to travel through the South by rail again. He arranged a tour that took "General Tom Thumb and Co.," as the troupe was now called, into the southern states and as far west as San Antonio, Texas.

During one of their stopovers, Bleeker received a letter from Barnum, which he promptly read to the four performers. "An idea has occurred to me," said the letter. "What do you think of a 'Tour Around the World'?"

The letter went on to name some of the countries that the traveling performers would visit—China, Japan, India, and Australia. It concluded with these instructions: "Talk it over with the 'little people.' Decide quickly! If you consent to undertake the journey, prepare to start next month."

A worldwide tour? Tom thought it a foolish idea. "Never! Never will I go to

Australia!" he said. "Why, it is upon the other side of the world."

Lavinia agreed. "Go to Australia?" she said. "Our friends would never expect to see us again. They would consider us dead and buried."

Bleeker, however, aware of Tom's fondness for wealth, managed to overcome the Thumbs' opposition to the idea. He did so by pointing out a paragraph in the letter about the gold mines of Australia. "Tell the General," Barnum had written, "he will be able to make more money than a horse can draw." The vision of a horse attempting to pull a massive amount of gold too heavy to move helped change Tom's mind about the tour.

On June 21, 1869, the General Tom Thumb Company left New York by train for San Francisco, where the troupe was to board a steamer for Yokohama, Japan. Besides the four principal performers, and Sylvester Bleeker and his wife, the tour group now included a treasurer, a pianist, a doorkeeper, and an assistant, as well as a groom and coachman for the ponies and miniature coach they were taking along.

The troupe offered a wide range of entertainment. They sang songs, danced, and did impersonations. They performed short theatrical scenes and comic skits. And they appeared in one glamorous outfit after another.

As Barnum had noted in his letter, a railroad line linking the Atlantic and Pacific coasts had recently begun operating. The "last spike" of the first transcon-

tinental railroad, in fact, had been driven only a few weeks earlier, on May 10, 1869, at Promontory Summit, Utah.

Armies of workers had been recruited, including thousands of Chinese immigrants, to lay the track, which stretched almost two thousand miles, some of it through land held by the Plains Indians. Indian raiding parties rustled livestock belonging to the railroad companies, terrorized work crews, and isolated station towns. Both Cheyenne and Sioux raiding parties attempted to derail trains on various occasions. In 1868, the Sioux were successful, upturning rails and causing a wreck that killed two crewmen.

In the days before Tom, Lavinia, and the others left on their cross-country trek, their friends warned them of such attacks. And once their train got beyond the Mississippi River and began crossing the Great Plains, they began to hear more stories of Indian violence.

Alarmed, Tom went to Bleeker and urged him to provide everyone in the group with a revolver. He even offered to pay for the weapons, whatever the cost. But to Bleeker it seemed unwise for any member of the group to wield a pistol. No one had experience with firearms. It would be asking for an accident. He said no to Tom's request.

A good number of the other passengers carried rifles. To demonstrate how well they could handle their weapons, they would fire them from the train windows from time to time, unnerving Tom and the others.

The passengers' careless gunshots proved to be the most frightening part of the trip. Though Tom and the other members of the cast did sight Indians on occasion, their train was never attacked.

After arriving in California, they performed in a number of small towns. On November 4, 1869, the members of the troupe, along with hundreds of other passengers, boarded the ocean liner *America*, bound for Yokohama, Japan.

Railroad travel was an unpleasant business in the 1860s. Passengers often had to sleep in their seats in the desperately crowded coaches. They froze in the winter, sweltered in the summer, and had to provide their own food. ✦ *New York Public Library*

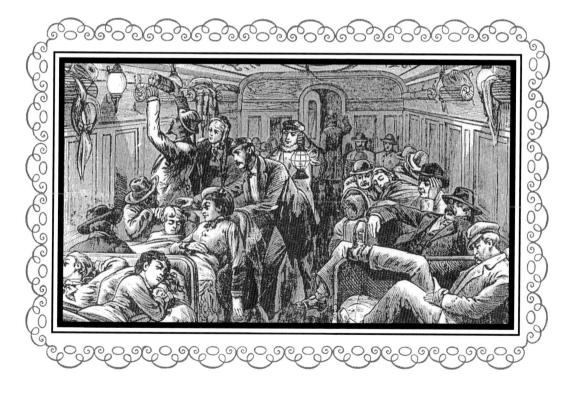

In Japan in the nineteenth century, Americans were a great rarity, and so, of course, Americans with dwarfism were something most Japanese had never seen. As a result, whenever Tom, Lavinia, the Commodore, and Minnie attempted to go sightseeing on the streets of Yokohama, people would rush from their homes and shops and follow them. The crowds, according to Lavinia, often numbered in the hundreds.

Tom was curious about the Japanese bathhouses because he had heard that men and women bathed together in the nude. When he and Bleeker visited a bathhouse, the manager took Tom by the hand and led him outside to the street, where he could view the bathers through a window and thereby not cause a disturbance. But the General was too short to see through the window. The manager then brought Tom back inside, where he stared at the men and women together in a mammoth swimming pool. Then the bathers noticed Tom. They pointed and shouted and scrambled out of the pool. Within seconds, Tom found himself surrounded by a clamorous crowd of naked men and women.

Tom was stunned. On the walk back to their hotel, he was very quiet. Later he said, "If we tell this to the folks back home, they will not believe us. But it is *so!*"

After Japan, the troupe sailed across the Yellow Sea to China. When they gave a performance at a huge theater in Shanghai, Lavinia later said, her songs brought "great applause," while the General's character sketches were received

with "open-mouthed wonder." It didn't seem to matter that their performances were in English.

From China, the troupe went to Hong Kong, Macao, and Singapore. After Singapore, they once again boarded a passenger liner and arrived in Australia on February 16, 1870. In Melbourne, the largest and most important city in Australia at the time, they performed in one of the city's biggest theaters. They drew loud cheers and applause from the overflowing audience. It was a madhouse. Lavinia recalled that "they filled the orchestra, they sat upon the stage, they hung upon the proscenium columns, they climbed from the galleries and sat upon the figures supporting the private boxes."

In Melbourne, Bleeker hired two stagecoaches to take the troupe to the town of Ballarat, a distance of about sixty-five miles northwest of the city. Thousands of gold seekers had flocked to Ballarat after the precious metal was discovered there in 1851. To mark their visit, Tom ordered a bracelet of native gold for Lavinia and had it engraved with the date: June 2, 1870.

The troupe remained in Ballarat for three weeks. While there, they visited an orphanage to entertain the children. Tom and the others soon learned that their popularity had preceded them. When they were brought before the children, one boy, about five years old, shouted out, "It's Tom Thumb and his wife, Commodore Nutt and Minnie Warren!"

Another exclaimed, "General Tom Thumb got married to Lavinia Warren by Barnum!"

Considering that Australia is halfway around the world from the United States, and communication between the two countries was—before radio, TV, and the Internet—infrequent at best, it was remarkable how far and fast the popularity of the cast members had spread.

General Tom Thumb & Co. spent nine months in Australia, traveling more than five thousand miles and performing in 105 cities and towns.

India was next. In Benares (now Varanasi), an Indian holy city, they called upon the king of Benares. The morning after the visit, two enormous elephants appeared outside the cottage in which Lavinia and Tom were staying. They were a gift from the king, who owned a huge elephant herd. The two he presented to the Thumbs were his favorites; he had ridden one of them on tiger hunts. Tom and Lavinia couldn't even begin to imagine what it would be like trying to travel the world with a pair of tiger-hunting elephants. They had to politely refuse the generous gift.

The troupe traveled more than thirty-five hundred miles in India, visiting Calcutta and Bombay (now Mumbai), as well as countless other cities and towns. From India, they sailed west on the steamship *Surat*, crossing the Indian Ocean to the port of Aden. Then it was north across the Red Sea to Egypt, where they

Their worldwide tour took Tom and his troupe to British India, where they were presented
to the king of Benares. ✦ *From* Gen. Tom Thumb's Three Years' Tour Around the World

performed in Cairo and Alexandria. From Alexandria, the troupe crossed the
Mediterranean to Italy. Not long after, Tom was back in England for the fourth
time.

On June 22, 1872, General Tom Thumb & Co. sailed into New York Harbor.

Toward the end of the worldwide tour, the stagecoach carrying Tom and his troupe was forced to cross a swollen river in northern Ireland. Water surged through the windows to the level of the seats, terrifying the passengers. Nonetheless, they reached the opposite shore safely. ✦ *From* Gen. Tom Thumb's Three Years' Tour Around the World

It had been three years and one day since their departure. They had traveled more than 55,000 miles and circled the globe. They had given performances in 587 cities and towns.

Tom and Lavinia were weary. They wanted to see their families and friends— and rest.

"We'll live in quiet Middleboro and just be happy," Tom said to Lavinia. "We have plenty of money, we have each other. What else matters?"

Superstar

OM AND LAVINIA did not rest for very long. Beginning in the fall of 1872, they resumed their travels. Barnum arranged a tour that took them across the continent to California a second time. According to Lavinia, they performed to "immense audiences." Everywhere they went, people wanted to talk to them about their worldwide travels.

Once the tour had ended and they were back home, Tom focused on having fun. That meant returning to his love of sailing and his big yacht, the *Maggie B.* Tom hired a captain to staff the vessel and get her "in racing trim," as he put it. He also hired a cook and a deck hand as crew members.

Tom proved his skill as a sailor by taking first prize at the Brooklyn Yacht Club regatta held at New London, Connecticut. He later won a second yacht race in a competition at Martha's Vineyard, Massachusetts.

When it wasn't his yacht that occupied him, it was his horses. He delighted in driving his matched pair of Shetland ponies over country roads. Tom also rode horseback. He bought a small chestnut gelding for himself and a tiny gray mare for Lavinia, who also enjoyed riding,

Lavinia became concerned about the large amounts of money Tom was spending. He had to borrow to purchase his yachts and horses and to enlarge the stable. He bought Lavinia beautiful clothes and expensive jewelry.

As their debts piled up, Lavinia protested, but only mildly. She could not bring herself to reproach Tom for his indulgences or deprive him of the pleasure that he got from giving.

Tom continued to grow steadily as an adult. By the early 1870s, he was in his midthirties and about the size of a stout five-year-old, at forty inches and seventy pounds. In fact, when he ordered custom-made suits but was not available for fittings, the tailor used Clarence Eddy, a presumably chubby five-year-old Bridgeport boy, as his substitute.

Tom was not only getting taller—he was growing emotionally too. He came to realize that his early life had been one of make-believe. To the public, he was General Tom Thumb off the stage as well as on it. He loved the privileged treatment and the adulation, of course. But there were times when he tired of playing the long-familiar roles. There were times when he wanted to be Charles S. Stratton again and be respected as an actor and entertainer, a person with talent.

In his performances, he stopped playing roles that required wearing childish costumes or girls' clothes. He now preferred to deliver informal lectures, telling his audiences of his international travels and encounters with European royalty.

Now that Tom was doing fewer impressions and comedy routines, he and Lavinia hired other acts, which gave their performances the character of a variety show. They usually offered a magician or a ventriloquist, plus Lavinia and other dwarfs who took part in comedy sketches.

Tom and Lavinia's celebrity had reached such a fevered pitch that paper dolls were created of the couple. ◆ *Bridgeport Public Library Historical Collection (Lavinia), Strong National Museum of Play (Tom)*

In 1874, Tom and Lavinia added to their troupe "Major" Edward Newell, a professional roller skater. He dazzled audiences with his fancy skating. He also sang, danced, and did impersonations. Newell was not considered a dwarf; he was merely very short. He was once described as "not quite" a dwarf. By today's standards, that would mean he was four feet, eleven inches or taller. While he was head and shoulders taller than Lavinia, she still referred to him as a "little man."

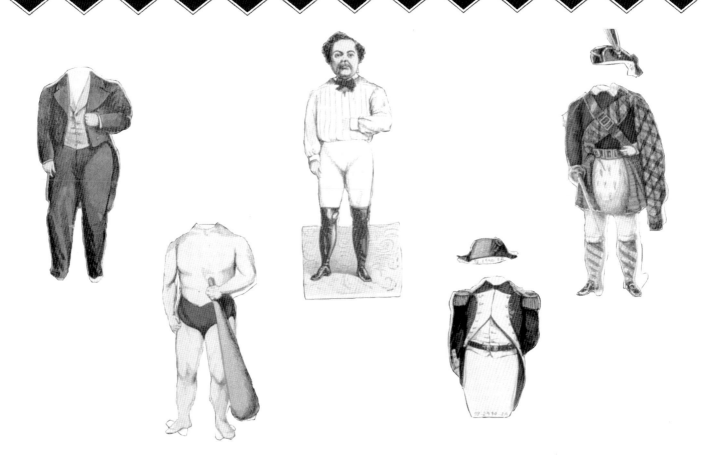

Three years later, Lavinia's sister Minnie married Newell. The couple moved in with the Thumbs in their spacious Middleboro home.

Early in 1878, Minnie announced she was having a baby. The Thumbs were delighted.

Minnie had been born a dwarf. Major Newell was nearly short enough to qualify as a person with dwarfism. They were convinced their baby would be very small. In those days, before ultrasounds and other modern medical technology, there was no good way of monitoring how Minnie's baby was growing, and she died painfully, giving birth to a full-size infant. The baby died too.

Minnie's death was almost more than Lavinia could bear. Since all of their brothers and other sisters were of average size, Lavinia and Minnie, feeling somewhat isolated from them, had developed a special closeness.

There was something else. Being taller and almost eight years older than Minnie, Lavinia had always felt an obligation to care for and protect her little sister. Minnie's death made Lavinia think that she had somehow failed in her responsibility, that maybe she could have said or done something that might have preserved her sister's life. That feeling deepened her grief.

To help them recover from this terrible blow, the Thumbs went back to touring. They took no cast members. It was just the two of them, plus a little black dog named Topsy. The Bleekers went with them. Mr. Bleeker managed the tour,

while Mrs. Bleeker, with whom Lavinia had developed a close friendship, again served as wardrobe mistress.

While the Thumbs were touring, Barnum entered their lives once more. Beginning in 1871, Barnum had been making a name for himself in the circus business. In 1880 he teamed up with the English showman James A. Bailey to form what he called "The Greatest Show on Earth." Barnum's circus was the first to travel by rail and the first to stage performances in more than one ring at a time. It was the forerunner of today's Ringling Bros. and Barnum & Bailey Circus.

Barnum enticed Tom and Lavinia to join the circus for the season of 1881 for what the showman promised would be "positively their last season of exhibition." As each performance opened, the Thumbs paraded about the Big Top, with the brass band, elephants, caged tigers, trained animals, trapeze artists, and clowns.

The Thumbs starred in the circus museum and sideshow with other acts and exhibits that Barnum had assembled. One of these was the original Fejee Mermaid, which Barnum had shamelessly once again brought back from obscurity.

The circus covered a big portion of the United States that season. It traveled east to Bangor, Maine, west to Omaha, Nebraska, and south to Galveston, Texas.

Although Barnum did all he could to make Tom and Lavinia comfortable, the circus was, all in all, a hellish experience for the couple. Train wrecks were a

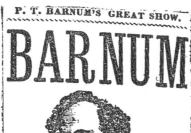

P. T. BARNUM'S GREAT SHOW.

BARNUM

I AM HERE!

At Lincoln Park!

WITH MY

Greatest Show on Earth!

Which is NOW OPEN, and

I will address the audience at each exhibition

AFTERNOON AND EVENING,

ALL THE TIME IT IS TO BE HERE.

---

3 DAYS ONLY,

Tuesday, Wednesday, and Thursday, Sept. 9, 10, and 11, Afternoon and Evening, and positively remains no longer.

Ten Thousand Visitors!

DAILY, AND HUNDREDS TURNED AWAY.

3 Grand Palace Pavilions!

WONDERFUL

TRAINED WILD BEASTS!

GRAND

ROMAN HIPPODROME!

MAMMOTH

MUSEUM

And the most refined, elegant, greatest, grandest, and most

Magnificent Circus!

EVER ORGANIZED.

20 TRAINED ROYAL STALLIONS!

In New and Wonderful Acts.

12 LEARNED ELEPHANTS!

Giants, Dwarfs, Automata, and Fifty Thousand Wonders in the Great Traveling Museum.

1,000 WILD BEASTS

100 PEERLESS PERFORMERS!

In the Colossal EQUESTRIAN COLLEGE, and

YOUTHFUL, DARING

8 LADY RIDERS!

DOORS OPEN at 1 and 7 p. m. Performances 2 and 8 p. m. ADMISSION, 50 cents. Children under 9, half price. Reserved Chairs, 25 cents extra. For the accommodation of ladies, children, and families, I have erected a **Spacious Elevated Platform, furnished with 2,000 Reserved Numbered Chairs,** which may be secured for any Exhibition at HAWLEY'S NEWS DEPOT, VINE STREET, at the usual slight advance, by those who desire to avoid the crowd on the grounds.

Ladies, children, and others wishing to avoid the crowd in the evening, are advised to attend the Afternoon Exhibitions.

It   P. T. BARNUM. Proprietor.

In typical high-spirited language, Barnum announces, "I Am Here!" in this circus advertisement, which appeared in a Cincinnati newspaper in 1879.

✦ *New York Public Library*

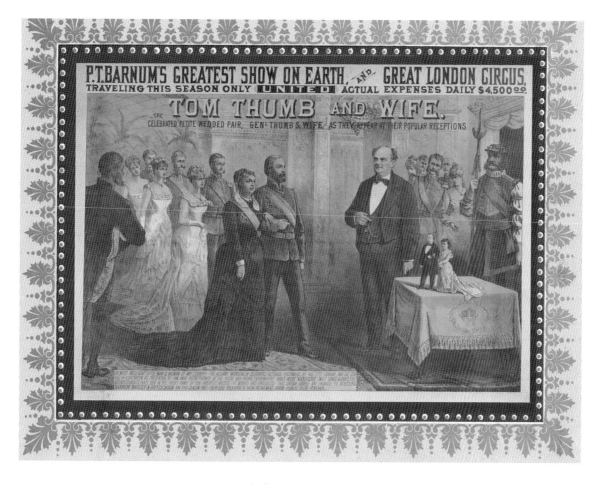

A circus poster promoting Barnum's "Greatest Show on Earth" depicts the Thumbs and
Barnum at a reception that the showman staged for the socially elite.
✦ *John and Mable Ringling Museum of Art*

scourge of the fast-developing rail system and its inexperienced crews. Tom and
Lavinia suffered as a result. They endured frightful collisions with other trains,
and on at least four occasions the railroad car in which Tom and Lavinia lived

ran off the tracks. Tom became very nervous. After one accident, he believed that he and Lavinia would "never get home safe."

They longed to be back in Middleboro. When the season was over, they told Barnum they were withdrawing from circus life and returned home.

After a quiet spell, they took up their travels again with the Bleekers. They were in Milwaukee on the night of January 10, 1883, when tragedy struck. After their performance that evening, Tom, Lavinia, and the Bleekers returned to their rooms in Newhall House, the six-story brick hotel where they were staying. Tom and Lavinia had a room on the third floor.

A few hours before dawn of the next morning, fire broke out in the hotel. Flames shot high into the night sky. Like most hotel guests, the Thumbs and the Bleekers were asleep when the fire trucks arrived and firefighters began placing ladders against the burning building. A pounding on the Thumbs' door awakened them. Tom opened it and a police officer rushed in. Smoke filled the room, and the Thumbs could hear the screams of other guests. The police officer opened a window, and the firefighters below raised a ladder to it. Tom went down the ladder first. The policeman followed, with Lavinia in his arms.

The Bleekers were not so fortunate. They were in their room on the fourth floor, directly above the Thumbs. No ladder appeared at their window. Mr. Bleeker cut a blanket into strips and made a crude lifeline, which he used to start lowering his wife to a balcony below. But she lost her grip and fell to the balcony,

fracturing her right leg and left arm and dislocating her left shoulder. She also suffered cuts and bruises. Mr. Bleeker managed to escape the building and give aid to his badly injured wife, but she died twelve days later, one of the seventy-one people who perished as a result of the blaze.

Tom sat stunned as flames reduced the building to ashes in what would be called one of the worst hotel fires in American history. He could only watch as Lavinia went among the injured and sought to comfort as many people as possible.

Tom never recovered from the shock of that horror-filled night. In the weeks that followed, he lived in a daze. Lavinia eventually began touring by herself, leaving Tom behind in Middleboro.

Tom was alone in his bedroom on the morning of July 15, 1883, when he suffered a stroke, the blockage of blood flow to the brain, and died. He was forty-five years old.

Lavinia, on tour, was in Cincinnati when the news of Tom's passing was brought to her. She rushed home.

On the morning of Tom's funeral, his body was exhibited at St. John's Episcopal Church in Bridgeport. When the church doors opened at ten o'clock, a great mass of people pressed their way in. Mothers brought their children for a final glimpse of the General.

An estimated ten thousand people tried to gain admittance to the funeral

later that afternoon. Those who could not enter the church stood in silence outside. Lavinia, dressed in black, a long veil covering her face, sat in the front pew, weeping quietly, her head resting on her mother's shoulder.

Barnum, who had been in Montreal when he got the news of Tom's passing, sat in the pew behind Lavinia, his head bowed.

At the nearby Mountain Grove Cemetery, another huge crowd awaited the arrival of the funeral procession. Lavinia sobbed loudly during the gravesite ceremonies, and at one point she fainted in her mother's arms.

Before he died, Tom had arranged for a life-size statue of himself to be sculpted out of marble. Following his wishes, the sculpture was mounted atop a forty-foot marble shaft and placed on his grave. The site was later vandalized; Tom's statue and the marble column lay in pieces. A second statue and a shorter column eventually replaced them.

In her autobiography, Lavinia said that her marriage to Tom was "a happy one" and that he was "kind, affectionate, and generous." But he was not always careful with money. He had squandered away much of the fortune the couple had accumulated on yachts, horses, and other playthings. He left Lavinia with some securities and jewelry, small pieces of property in Brooklyn, and slightly

This 1881 photograph is one of the last taken of Tom and Lavinia together. Tom was forty-three; Lavinia, forty. ✦ *Bridgeport Public Library Historical Collection*

more than $16,000 in the bank. Though not a small amount in those days (about $350,000 in today's money), it would not support Lavinia in the manner to which she'd become accustomed.

Before Tom's death, Lavinia hoped to retire and return to private life. She worried that it might not be possible now.

Lavinia was still very much in demand. She received letters from carnival owners and theater managers almost daily, offering her work. In spite of her growing concerns about money, Lavinia said no to all of the proposals.

Then one day several months after Tom's death, Lavinia traveled to Bridgeport to visit Sylvester Bleeker and other friends. Barnum was another guest. When they spoke, Lavinia asked him whether she should retire. The seventy-three-year-old Barnum had strong opinions on the subject. He told Lavinia that she belonged to the public, and if the public wanted to see her, she should follow their wishes.

He reminded Lavinia and Bleeker that he had retired at the age of sixty-two. Three years of unhappiness followed. Barnum said, "No doubt if I continued to be inactive I would have died."

Turning to Bleeker, Barnum declared, "Take her out! Take her out!"

Lavinia followed Barnum's advice and returned to the stage in 1884. Her performances now included two Italian little people—Count Primo Magri, who

A life-size statue of Charles Stratton crowns his gravesite monument at the Mountain Grove Cemetery. ◆ *George Sullivan*

was an inch taller than Lavinia, and his brother Ernesto Magri, who was about the same size. For a brief time before Tom's passing, they had been members of the General's troupe.

The Count sang and played the piano and a small flute called a piccolo. The Baron, who also sang, was a professional whistler, sometimes accompanying his brother. His whistle was a great convenience, he said, since it "takes no room in packing."

On the road, the two brothers performed selections from operas. Lavinia thought the public would prefer "catchy" tunes rather than operas in a foreign language. She may have been right. The company never came close to achieving the popularity that Tom and his cast had enjoyed.

In New York on April 6, 1885, about two years after Tom's death, Lavinia and Count Magri were married. Only personal friends were invited. Lavinia's only comment on the ceremony was that there was "no disagreeable crowding."

After the marriage, Lavinia, the Count, and the Baron went back to touring. But their fortunes went downhill. Lavinia had to rent out the house in Middleboro that she and Tom had built. She and the Count moved across the street to live with Lavinia's brother in what had once been their parents' home.

As Lavinia entered her sixties, she and the Count continued to perform.

Photographed while on tour in Chicago not long after Tom's passing, Lavinia wears mourning clothes of a stylish cut. ✦ *Bridgeport Public Library Historical Collection*

In 1885, Lavinia married a second time, taking Count Primo Magri as her husband.
He, along with his brother Baron Ernesto Magri, had earlier been members
of Tom Thumb's troupe. ✦ *The Barnum Museum*

They appeared in sideshows and at country fairs. And when vaudeville came along in the 1880s, Lavinia and the Count fit right in. Vaudeville is a form of entertainment offering several separate, unrelated variety acts—singers, dancers, comedians, impersonators, acrobats, jugglers, and magicians—on a single program, or "bill." It was made to order for Lavinia's and the Count's talents.

Lavinia was sometimes asked, "Don't you get tired of this public life?" She always had the same response: "I belong to the public. The appearing before audiences has been my life. I've hardly known any other."

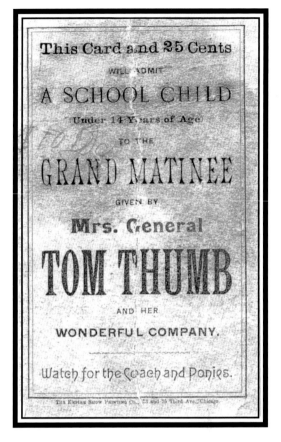

With this card, Lavinia and her "Wonderful Company" made a special twenty-five-cent offer to schoolchildren of the time. ✦ *Author's collection*

If Lavinia ever thought seriously about withdrawing from public life, all she had to do was speak to Barnum. "Keep going, Mrs. Stratton," he would tell her. "Keep going."

In 1891, Barnum passed away. He was eighty years old. And he "died in harness," as Lavinia put it, meaning that he kept to his usual routine until the

very end. In his final days, Barnum was giving interviews to the newspapers and issuing orders concerning his funeral arrangements. The showman was buried at the Mountain Grove Cemetery in a gravesite across the road from Tom's.

The nineteenth century wound down, and early in the 1900s, Lavinia and the Count began to spend their summers as performers at Lilliputia at New York's Coney Island. Lilliputia was a "midget city," a complete village scaled in size to accommodate some three hundred dwarfs who had been hired away from circuses and carnival sideshows.

As spectators gaped, citizens of Lilliputia went about their daily lives: shopping in miniature stores, going to a miniature theater, taking a dip in the ocean under the watchful eyes of lifeguards seated on their miniature lifeguard stands. Coney Island had offered its first freak show in 1880 and in the years that followed exhibited more human oddities than any other place in the world. Lilliputia was among its greatest successes. But in 1911, much of Coney Island's amusement area went up in flames, and Lilliputia disappeared with it.

After Coney Island, Lavinia and the Count traveled to Hollywood, which had recently replaced the East Coast as the center of the fast-growing movie industry. In 1914, Lavinia and the Count appeared in *The Lilliputians' Courtship*, a silent film. Lavinia was cast as Lady Petite, the Count as Uncle Tiny Mite.

Once the rigors of travel became too difficult for the couple, they settled down in Middleboro. There they opened Primo's Pastime, a small store that

Although photos from the Coney Island Lilliputia are exceedingly rare, other groups of dwarfs in the late 1800s and early 1900s sometimes appeared on stage together. This group, pictured playing cards, was also dubbed "The Lilliputians." The original Lilliputians were six–inch–tall inhabitants of Lilliput, an island in Jonathan Swift's novel *Gulliver's Travels.* ✦ *Special Collections Research Center, Syracuse University Library.*

offered snacks, soft drinks, and their own autographed photographs.

On October 31, 1919, Lavinia was spirited enough to entertain over 150 guests in celebration of her seventy-eighth birthday. But in the days after the party, Lavinia became seriously ill. She died at her home on November 25, 1919. She was buried next to her first husband at Mountain Grove Cemetery, her grave marked by a small stone that read, simply, WIFE.

Even during the time she was married to Count Magri, Lavinia was generally known as Tom Thumb's widow. She knew well the drawing power of Tom's name. Lavinia, Count Magri, his brother, and the other performers with whom they toured were usually billed as "Mrs. Tom Thumb and Her Wonderful Company." And while she signed souvenir photographs as "Countess Lavinia Magri," she frequently added "Mrs. General Tom Thumb."

Tom Thumb's name still carries a mystique and a certain appeal. There's Tom Thumb lettuce, Tom Thumb doughnuts, and a Tom Thumb rose, and the name has been adopted by miniature golf courses. Tom Thumb is the name of a convenience store chain in the southeast and a string of supermarkets in Texas. Although some of the allusions might also refer to the traditional hero of English folklore, our culture has not forgotten the "real" Tom Thumb.

Tom Thumb's marriage to Lavinia Warren in 1863, which was so lavishly reported, has also inspired special tribute. During the 1920s, a new fad arose: Tom Thumb weddings. In these events small children played the roles of bride and

Like countless other enterprises in the United States, this Bridgeport florist shop has been named in Tom Thumb's honor. ✦ *George Sullivan*

groom and other members of the wedding party. In some such "weddings" the children received "certificates of marriage" as mementos. The practice continues today, though less frequently, usually as a fundraiser for churches and other community organizations. Guests buy tickets to attend the event, with the money realized going to the designated charity.

Tom Thumb and Lavinia's marriage was the inspiration for mock weddings with children acting out the roles of bride and groom, as depicted here in this nineteenth-century photograph. There are still Tom Thumb weddings held today, often as fundraising events. ♦ *J. W. & J. S. Moulton, Collection of Jack and Beverly Wilgus*

One incident, in particular, illustrates how the world viewed Tom Thumb. When Barnum and Tom were in Paris in 1844, Tom appeared for the first time in *Le Petit Poucet.* Tom sang, danced, and performed as an actor. He won enthusiastic praise from Paris newspaper critics as well the French acting community.

Afterward, when Tom and Barnum were leaving France, and thereby subject to an exit tax, French authorities asked Tom to pay a "theatrical tax." This was considerably less than the "natural curiosities tax," which was normally imposed upon a freak show performer.

During the nineteenth century, countless men and women of short stature found employment in the entertainment field. Many were put on exhibit in carnival sideshows or circuses. Some performed on stage, but none came close to equaling Tom's prominence. Their most distinctive quality was their dwarfism.

But Tom, from the time he first performed at Barnum's American Museum as a five-year-old, was a notable achiever, and eventually he became the most prominent stage performer of the day, not only in America but around the world. This was no small achievement in a time before global mass media. He was a true celebrity in the modern sense of the word, in an era when there were few—and the first Little Person to earn not only recognition but respect, to be seen not merely as a curiosity but as a person.

ACKNOWLEDGMENTS

I am very grateful to the many people who helped me in my research on this book and aided me in gathering the photographs and other illustrations. Special thanks are due Mary K. Witkowski, head of Historical Collections at the Bridgeport Public Library, and the librarian Elizabeth Van Tuyl, who permitted me to sift through and study the library's impressive collection of material pertaining to Tom Thumb and P. T. Barnum. I had a similar opportunity at the Barnum Museum in Bridgeport, thanks to the executive director Kathy Maher and the collections manager Alessandra Wood.

Special thanks to Dorothy Thayer of the Middleboro Historical Museum in Middleboro, Massachusetts; Gina Halkias-Seugling of the General Research Division of the New York Public Library; Betty Adelson for her wise counsel; Ethan Crough, who vetted the manuscript; Gillian Alcatara, Sandy Becker, and Gary Arnold, Little People of America; Nicolette A. Dobrowolski, head of Public Services, and Kathleen Manwaring, Special Collections Research Center, Syracuse University Library; Jesse Christian, Tibbals digital collection manager, Ringling Museum of Art; Pamela Madsen, Harvard Theatre Collection; Tom Harris, who reignited my interest in this project at a crucial time; Bill Sullivan, for his research in Oxford, Connecticut; Michael Chemers, assistant professor of dramatic literature, Carnegie Mellon University; Jon Mann, editor and publisher, *The Rail Splitter*; Armand Chevette, director, Mountain Grove Cemetery Association; Athena Angelos, photograph researcher, Washington, D.C.; Raphael David, M.D., N.Y.U. Medical Center; Charles Schwartz, John Strong, and art director Christine Kettner, who put her heart and soul and uncommon expertise into this project.

I'm also deeply grateful to Jennifer Greene, my editor at Clarion Books, for her comments that helped to shape the book's matter and meaning, and her diligence and persistence in seeking to achieve a perfectly accurate manuscript. Thank you, Jennifer.

Tom stepping out of his miniature carriage. ✦ *London Stereoscopic Company/Getty Images*

Several sections of this book, the early chapters in particular, are based at least in part on primary source material in the form of autobiographical texts, booklets, theatrical programs, letters, and diaries kindly made available to me at the New-York Historical Society, the Bridgeport Public Library, and the Barnum Museum in Bridgeport. The various editions of Barnum's autobiography were important to me, even though the pages devoted exclusively to "The General," as Barnum usually called Tom, were relatively few in number. Anything written by Barnum had to be regarded with some caution, however, considering the showman's penchant for stretching the truth in his desire to manipulate public opinion. *The Autobiography of Mrs. Tom Thumb*, another good source, had its own shortcomings. Lavinia Thumb often relied on passages taken from Barnum's autobiography and from Sylvester Bleeker's *Gen. Tom Thumb's Three Years' Tour Around the World*. She in fact lifted large amounts of text from the Bleeker book. A. H. Saxon's wide-ranging and insightful introduction enhanced the value of Lavinia's book.

In appraising secondary sources, it should be noted that only a small handful of books have been written about Charles Sherwood Stratton, although he was a person of renown and, as General Tom Thumb, one of the nation's first show business notables, a genuine "name." *Barnum Presents General Tom Thumb* was the best of what's available. The author Alice Curtis Desmond lived in Bridgeport for many years, and among her friends were descendants and relatives of P. T. Barnum and his family. To Mrs. Desmond, Tom Thumb was "a hometown boy." Besides having an intimate knowledge of the Stratton family, she had her manuscript fact-checked by surviving relatives of the Barnum and Stratton families.

In the case of Barnum himself, I turned to A. H. Saxon's thoroughly researched *P. T. Barnum: The Legend and the Man*, the closest thing I could find for an authentic portrait of the complex showman. On the subject of dwarfism, I leaned on *The Lives of Dwarfs: Their Journey from Public Curiosity Toward Social Liberation* by Betty Adelson. Ms. Adelson treated the subject with sensitivity and vision.

Notes

INTRODUCTION

"decently and in order . . .": *New York Times*, February 11, 1863, p. 8.

"He was a genius in promotion . . .": *New York Times*, November 9, 2007, p. 31.

1. A MAN IN MINIATURE

"I love to watch children play . . .": Desmond, p. 10.

"He's here! He's here!": Desmond, p. 8.

"No, I can't . . .": Desmond, p. 8.

"I'm going straight over . . .": Desmond, p. 8.

"Remarkable. Taylor won't believe this . . .": Desmond, p. 11.

"What did you say about . . .": Desmond, p. 12.

2. PRINCE OF HUMBUGS

"I wanted an opportunity . . .": Barnum (1855), p. 143.

"I had long fancied . . .": Barnum (1855), p. 143.

"Young Indian chiefs . . .": Bogdan, p. 31.

"was the slave of Augustine Washington . . .": Barnum (1855), p. 153.

"[A] greater object of marvel . . .": Kunhardt, p. 20.

"I raised him": Thomson, p. 103.

"nurse of Washington": Kunhardt, p. 23.

"putting on glittering appearances . . .": Saxon, p. 31.

"representatives of the wonderful": Kunhardt, p. 234.

"the smallest child I ever saw . . .": Barnum (1855), p. 243.

"Charles S. Stratton, son of . . .": Barnum (1855), p. 243.

"He was a bright-eyed little fellow . . .": Barnum (1855), p. 243.

3. MAKEOVER

"Show Charley with those freaks?": Desmond, p. 13.

"P. T. Barnum of the American Museum . . .": Desmond, p. 19.

"contained two deceptions": Barnum (1855), p. 243.

"It would have been . . .": Barnum (1855), p. 243.

"a fancy for European exotics": Barnum (1855), p. 244.

"Nothing so small or fairy-like . . .": *Sketch of the Life*, p. 5.

"He became very fond of me . . .": Barnum (1855), pp. 244, 245.

4. ON STAGE

"I may be billed hereafter . . .": *Sketch of the Life*, p. 7.

"a good sized dog": Kunhardt, p. 110.

"Ladies and Gentleman . . .": Desmond, p. 51.

"and he fairly earned it": Barnum (1855), p. 245.

"impossible to prevent his doing": Desmond, p. 62.

"Were he deformed or sickly . . .": Desmond, p. 63.

"Young man . . .": Desmond, p. 64.

"On one day . . .": Desmond, p. 65.

5. COMMAND PERFORMANCE

"Yes, I'm returning . . .": Desmond, p. 67.

"Oh, for the life on the ocean wave . . .": *Sketch of the Life*, p. 15.

"SMALLEST PERSON that ever . . .": Fleming, p. 54.

"Dear Mr. Barnum . . .": Desmond, p. 77.

"I am only a *Thumb* . . .": Desmond, p. 78.

"Is he really only . . .": Desmond, p. 81.

"Good Evening, Ladies and Gentlemen!": Desmond, p. 85.

"first rate": Desmond, p. 86.

"After dinner, we saw the greatest curiosity . . .": Saxon, p. 132.

"was born in [18]32 . . .": Saxon, p. 132.

"General, this is the Prince of Wales . . .": Barnum (1855), p. 260.

"Darling, what do you like to do best?": Desmond, p. 91.

"What d'you say?": Desmond, p. 92.

6. A ROYAL TREAT

"That is a very pretty song . . .": Barnum (1855), p. 261.

"I know this will make you happy . . .": Desmond, p. 95.

"It will be the greatest hit . . .": Kunhardt, p. 60.

"I declare, I've forgotten my pocketbook . . .": Desmond, p. 106.

"Wouldn't the keeper let us ride . . .": Desmond, p. 107.

"You're sure you have . . .": Desmond, p. 107.

"I'm General Thumb, just come to town . . .": Desmond, p. 128.

"The little General gave . . .": Goldfarb, p. 270.

"stage tact and comic humor": Goldfarb, p. 270.

"I have traveled . . .": Desmond, p. 171.

7. GROWING UP

"cuter than ever . . .": Saxon, p. 151.

"For thirteen years . . .": Desmond, p. 172.

"General Tom Thumb performed admirably . . .": Goldfarb, p. 270.

"an American institution . . .": Chemers [2004], p. 19.

"My Dear Mr. Barnum . . .": Kunhardt, p. 125.

"the same rollicking . . .": Desmond, p. 179.

"BARNUM IS ON HIS FEET AGAIN": Kunhardt, p. 136.

8. LAVINIA

"I should like to marry . . .": Desmond, p. 184.

"anxious to be obedient . . .": *Mrs. Tom Thumb*, p. 38.

"floating palace of curiosities": *Mrs. Tom Thumb*, p. 39.

"out West . . .": *Mrs. Tom Thumb*, pp. 39, 40.

"be looked upon . . .": *Mrs. Tom Thumb*, p. 49.

"full, round dimpled face . . .": *Mrs. Tom Thumb*, p. 51.

"Mr. Barnum, that is the most . . .": Barnum (1870), pp. 586, 587.

"to take time to think of it . . .": Barnum (1870), p. 587.

"So you're going . . ." to "Yes, Tom, you may . . .": Barnum (1870), pp. 593–96.

"I have felt . . .": Kunhardt, p. 165.

"crowded to suffocation": Barnum (1870), p. 601.

"Not for fifty thousand dollars": Barnum (1870), p. 603.

"She is a charming little creature . . .": Barnum (1870), 601.

"prettiness, brightness, and grace": *Harper's Weekly*, p. 477.

"Mother, isn't it funny . . .": *Mrs. Tom Thumb*, p. 62.

"a season of hurry and excitement": *Mrs. Tom Thumb*, p. 63.

"Truly it was a story . . .": *Mrs. Tom Thumb*, p. 63.

9. TOURING TOGETHER

"We'll go, won't we darling?": Desmond, p. 203.

"An idea has occurred to me . . .": *Mrs. Tom Thumb*, p. 97.

"Never! Never will I . . .": Bleeker, p. 9.

"Tell the General . . .": Bleeker, p. 10.

"If we tell this to the folks . . .": Bleeker, p. 62.

"open-mouthed wonder": *Mrs. Tom Thumb*, p. 123.

"they filled the orchestra . . .": *Mrs. Tom Thumb*, p. 141.

"It's Tom Thumb and his wife . . .": *Mrs. Tom Thumb*, p. 142.

"We'll live in quiet Middleboro . . .": Desmond, 209.

10. SUPERSTAR

"immense audiences": *Mrs. Tom Thumb*, p. 196.

"in racing trim": Desmond, p. 212.

"little man": *Mrs. Tom Thumb*, p. 169.

"positively their last season . . .": Kunhardt, p. 275.

"never get home safe": Saxon, p. 285.

"a happy one . . .": *Mrs. Tom Thumb*, pp. 169, 170.

"No doubt if I continued . . .": *Mrs. Tom Thumb*, p. 170.

"takes no room . . .": *Mrs. Tom Thumb*, p. 172.

"no disagreeable crowding": *Mrs. Tom Thumb*, p. 170.

"Don't you get tired . . .": Bogdan, p. 161.

"died in harness": *Mrs. Tom Thumb*, p. 173.

❂ BIBLIOGRAPHY ❂

Books by and About Tom Thumb and Lavinia Warren

Bleeker, Sylvester. *Gen. Tom Thumb's Three Years' Tour Around the World, Accompanied by His Wife—Lavinia Warren Stratton, Commodore Nutt, Miss Minnie Warren, and Party.* New York: S. Booth, [1872].

Desmond, Alice Curtis. *Barnum Presents General Tom Thumb.* New York: Macmillan, 1854.

Hunt, Mabel Leigh. *"Have You Seen Tom Thumb?"* Philadelphia, New York: Fredrick Stokes Company, 1942.

Magri, Countess M. Lavinia (Mrs. General Tom Thumb). *The Autobiography of Mrs. Tom Thumb: (Some of My Life Experiences).* Hamden, Conn.: Archon Books, 1979.

Romaine, Mertie E. *General Tom Thumb and His Lady.* Taunton, Mass.: William S. Sullwood Publishing, 1976.

Sketch of the Life, Personal Appearance, Character and Manners of Charles S. Stratton the Man in Miniature, Known as General Tom Thumb; also General Tom Thumb's Songs. New York: Van Norden & Amerman, 1847.

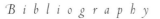

Bibliography

Books and Articles

Adams, Rachel. *Sideshow U.S.A.: Freaks and the American Cultural Imagination.* Chicago: University of Chicago Press, 2001.

Adelson, Betty M. *The Lives of Dwarfs: Their Journey from Public Curiosity Toward Social Liberation.* New Brunswick, N.J.: Rutgers University Press, 2005.

Barnum, Phineas T. *The Life of P. T. Barnum, Written by Himself.* New York: Redfield, 1855.

———. *The Humbugs of the World: An Account of Humbugs, Delusions, Impositions, Quackeries, Deceits and Deceivers Generally, in All Ages.* New York: Carle Tow, 1865.

———. *Struggles and Triumphs; or, Forty Years of Recollections of P. T. Barnum, Written by Himself.* Hartford: J. B. Burr, 1870.

Bogdan, Robert. *Freak Show: Presenting Human Oddities for Amusement and Profit.* Chicago: University of Chicago Press, 1988.

Chemers, Michael M. "Jumpin' Tom Thumb: Charles Stratton Onstage at the American Museum." *Nineteenth Century Theatre & Film* 31, no. 2 (December 2004): 16–27.

———. *Staging Stigma: A Critical Examination of the American Freak Show.* New York: Palgrave Macmillan, 2008.

Fleming, Alice. *P. T. Barnum: The World's Greatest Showman.* New York: Walker & Co., 1993.

Goldfarb, Alvin. "Gigantic and Minuscule Actors on the Nineteenth-Century American Stage." *Journal of Popular Culture* 10, no. 2 (1976): 264–79. Published online March 5, 2004.

Hornung, Clarence P. *The Way It Was: New York, 1850–1890.* New York: Shocken Books, 1977.

Kennedy, Dan. *Little People: Learning to See the World Through My Daughter's Eyes.* Emmaus, Pa.: Rodale Books, 2003.

Kunhardt, Philip B., Jr., Philip B. Kunhardt III, Peter W. Kunhardt. *P. T. Barnum: America's Greatest Showman.* New York: Alfred A. Knopf, 1995.

Presbrey, Frank. *The History and Development of Advertising.* Garden City, N.Y.: Doubleday, Doran & Co., 1929.

Roth, Hy, and Robert Cromie. *The Little People.* New York: Everest House, 1980.

Saxon, A. H. *P. T. Barnum: The Legend and the Man.* New York: Columbia University Press, 1989.

"Tom Thumb." *Harper's Weekly,* July 28, 1883, p. 477.

Thomson, Rosemarie Garland, editor. *Freakery: Cultural Spectacles of the Extraordinary Body.* New York: New York University Press, 1996.

Index

Page numbers in **bold** indicate illustrations.

Index

Front and back case:
Paper dolls created in the likeness
of General Tom Thumb
and his wife, Lavinia.

✦

Bridgeport Public Library Historical Collection
(Lavinia), Strong National Museum of Play (Tom)

Frontispiece:
Tom Thumb standing
on the hand of a soldier.

✦

London Stereoscopic Company / Getty Images

Page 202:
Mr. and Mrs. Tom Thumb
in later years.

✦

Author's collection